HOW TO WORK WITH JUNIORS
in the Sunday School

How to Work
with Juniors

in the Sunday School

Lillian Moore Rice

1147

Convention Press

NASHVILLE · TENNESSEE

© 1956 · Convention Press
Nashville, Tennessee

Printed in the United States of America
15. D 55 R.R.D.

About the Author

OF HER background experience in Junior work, Mrs. Rice says, "I began teaching Juniors when I was little more than an Intermediate (much too young for such a responsible task, of course), and I have spent all the years since working with that age exclusively.

"Ours was a one-room church building in those days, and my first class met in the little dark rectangle between pulpit and baptistry. We lacked everything in the way of material equipment, maps, pictures, tables, chalkboard—all the teaching aids that today we know are right and good. I learned early and I learned through hard experience the importance of using activities in guiding the learning of Juniors, and the teacher's need for guidance in using activities.

"As I grew up, so did our Sunday school. Soon we were departmentized, in a new building, and I was the Junior superintendent. The responsibility for finding, enlisting, and training teachers brought some experiences that I thought might be shared with others, so I wrote a few articles for *The Junior Teacher*. Soon I was asked to write Sunday school lessons for Juniors, Uniform Lessons first, then Graded Lessons. In 1944 I came to Nashville to become superintendent of Junior work for the Baptist Sunday School Board."

Mrs. Rice grew up and lived most of her life in Decatur, Georgia. She attended Agnes Scott College, Oglethorpe University, and studied Creative Writing and Journalism at the University of Georgia Extension School. Since coming to Nashville she has studied at Peabody College in the field of Elementary Education.

The Sunday School Training Course

THE Sunday School Training Course prepared by the Sunday School Department of the Baptist Sunday School Board is one of the major means of promoting Sunday school work. Its influence is limited only by its use.

The six sections of the course include studies in Bible, doctrines, evangelism, Sunday school leadership and administration, teaching, age group studies, and special studies. The range of the course is broad, for the field of Sunday school work is broad and requires comprehensive and specific training. Sixteen books are required for the completion of each Diploma.

The study of the training course is not to be limited to the present Sunday school workers. Most churches need twice as many workers as are now enlisted. This need can be supplied by training additional workers now. Members of the Young People's and Adult classes and older Intermediates should be led to study these books, for thereby will their service be assured. Parents will find help as they study what the Sunday school is trying to do.

Special Note to Instructors

During your teaching of this book will you check with the Sunday school superintendent and see if an accurate record of training for the workers is kept? If not, please urge him to set up such a file with an associate superintendent of training in charge. File cards for this purpose may be ordered at nominal cost from your nearest Baptist Book Store.

A. V. WASHBURN
Secretary, Teaching and Training
Sunday School Department
Baptist Sunday School Board

Contents

The Sunday School Training Course................ vii

1. Welcome, New Junior!............................   1

2. What Are They Like—the Juniors We Guide?.........   5

3. Grouping Juniors for Learning, Sharing, Worshiping..   21

4. The Right Workers for Juniors......................   34

5. Men and Women at Work...........................   49

6. A Good Sunday Morning for Juniors................   64

7. What is Good Teaching for Juniors?................   83

8. More Than Sunday Work........................... 101

9. Working with Parents of Juniors................... 112

10. The Environment Teaches, Too..................... 126

Questions for Review and Examination............. 139

Directions for the Teaching and Study
    of This Book for Credit........................ 142

Chapter 1

Welcome, New Junior!

JERRY STOPPED and read the three words over the door, "Welcome, New Juniors." Did he imagine it, or had he grown a little taller in the last minute? "New Juniors"—that meant him, Jerry Mason, age nine years and two months as of this Promotion Day. The certificate in his hand said it was true, and so did his Bible, the new *Junior* Bible his church had presented him in honor of the milestone he reached today.

It was a good feeling, being promoted. Jerry felt excited, expectant, eager to get inside the door and start doing whatever it was that Juniors did.

He could hear the "old Juniors" singing now. "Happy welcome to you," they sang. Jerry and the other Primary graduates stepped across the threshold.

It was a short step—it took only a second—but symbolically it was one of the longest of Jerry's Sunday school life. For with that step Jerry went from a level of Sunday school work planned around the needs of young children to a new level—one fitted to the more mature abilities and interests of late childhood.

"I want you to meet with your new teacher for a little while," the Junior superintendent told Jerry and the other Juniors. Then she added, "There will not be time for a lesson this morning."

She was wrong. Jerry did get a lesson that morning. So many things he saw and heard spelled out one big truth, one he had been privately hoping he would learn. *Being a Junior was different from being a Beginner or a Primary.*

Jerry's teacher, Mr. Brown, symbolized one important "new thing." When Mr. Brown had visited him the week be-

1

fore Promotion Day, Jerry had discovered that Junior boys had men for teachers, and that seemed a fine thing.

Sunday school was not something for boys just while they were boys, but for boys when they grew to be men like Mr. Brown.

Something else was different. All Jerry's classmates were boys. *Boys were in boys' classes taught by men. Girls were in girls' classes taught by women.*

Jerry went on making discoveries.

"I see that all of you have Bibles this morning," said Mr. Brown, calling attention to his pupils' gift-Bibles. "I hope you will have them next Sunday and all the Sundays to come. Do you know why your church has given you these Bibles?"

The reason, Jerry learned through discussion, was that a Junior studied his *own* lesson from his *own* Bible. In preparation for Sunday morning, Jerry was to read his lesson at home in the quarterly and in the Bible. In addition he was to read the Bible every day. Then on Sunday everybody brought Bibles to Sunday school because, as Mr. Brown explained, "We are always looking up things; and this year we are going to find out all sorts of interesting things—but you'll need Bibles to find them."

At home and at Sunday school, then, a Junior used his own Bible.

Next, Mr. Brown wrote a question on the board: "When is Sunday school over for a Junior?" The answer was surprising: "When the preaching service is ended." "Juniors do not go home when Sunday school is over," said Mr. Brown. "They go into the preaching service. Church time is a fine time to learn interesting things, use our minds, talk to God through singing and praying—"

So a Junior was expected to attend church services every Sunday. More than that, a Junior was old enough to take part in the services.

In the days and weeks that followed, Jerry was reminded many times of the larger responsibilities, the more mature activities involved in being a Junior.

One Saturday early in October, Mr. Brown had the boys in

his home to decide on a class name and to choose the jobs they wanted to do in the class. Some of the responsibility for keeping up class attendance, Jerry found, for getting the other boys to attend preaching, for planning outings, for gathering class news for the department paper was assumed by the Juniors themselves with the help of their teacher.

Many of the activities planned and carried out by the teacher of younger children were done by the Juniors in a Junior class.

There was something else that Jerry was to notice increasingly with the passing of the months. The teaching about Jesus took a new direction. More and more Jerry became aware of God's love that made him send Jesus, of Jesus' love that made him lay down his life for all the world. Jerry gradually came to believe that the most important decision anybody ever makes is to accept the gift that Jesus gave, to trust Jesus as Lord and Saviour, and to spend the rest of his life learning how to be a good follower.

A Junior, Jerry learned, is old enough to decide for himself what he thinks of Jesus; old enough to choose whether or not he will be his follower.

Every October tens of thousands of boys and girls discover, as Jerry did, that being promoted to the Junior department means more than being promoted to a new department, a new grade, a new teacher. It means being promoted to Sunday school work on a new size and scale—to new directions, new emphases, new demands on thinking and doing.

If we examine Jerry's discoveries, we will find the most important ways in which the Sunday school program is changed for boys and girls as they enter the Junior years.

In Junior years

1. Men teach boys and women teach girls.
2. For the class period—and for that period only—boys and girls are divided. (In all other activities—assemblies, department socials and outings—boys and girls worship and study, work and play together.)

3. Juniors use their Bibles in class on Sunday morning, in the assembly, and in home study.
4. Juniors are helped to form the habit of regular church attendance and, more than that, to participate in the service by listening, by thinking, by worshiping, sometimes by choosing.
5. In Junior classes Juniors themselves perform many of the tasks. They call absentees, work for good attendance, plan socials, arrange and decorate the room.
6. Since Junior boys and girls are old enough to make a decision for Christ, Junior teachers seek prayerfully to help them commit their hearts and ways and their whole long futures to him.

Chapter 2

What Are They Like—the Juniors We Guide?

ANY BOOK written to help men and women understand Junior Sunday school work must begin with a close-up study of Juniors, for that is where Junior Sunday school work begins. All we do for Juniors in the Sunday school—the kind of rooms we build, the type of lessons we provide, the way we group boys and girls for studying and worshiping—must fit the Junior, or those things are not right.

I. DISCOVERING OUR JUNIORS

Educators tell us that in guiding children a teacher has to borrow one practice of a good cabinetmaker. He must look for the grain of the wood; then work *with*, not *against*, the grain. That is another way of saying that teachers must try to understand the way God made boys and girls, must study the laws of growth (and the laws of human growth are God's laws as surely as the moral laws are his)—then work in harmony with those laws, not against them. A good parent said recently, "Maybe we would not be so concerned with the question, 'What kind of problem has this child got?' if we began at the right end and asked, 'What kind of child has this problem got?'"

We all understand that the only way to know Jerry is to study Jerry—to listen as he talks, to observe what he does, to weigh the home setting until slowly, surely, Jerry comes through with all the lights and shadings of his special personality.

But Jerry's teacher will have a better background for understanding this particular nine-year-old if he also has an understanding of nine-year-oldness. And Sandra's teacher is more apt to understand Sandra's ways if she knows something of the interests and abilities of other twelve-year-olds.

That is why we are devoting a chapter to a thoughtful study of Juniors, to the characteristics, problems, and needs of many boys and girls as observed and reported by many teachers.

1. Study of Juniors Was Long Neglected

For years students paid little attention to the study of late childhood. Infancy and early childhood were known to be periods of critical importance, and so was adolescence; but the Junior period was considered a strip of flat land, a sort of plateau between more colorful and eventful periods of life.

In the last few years, however, the picture has changed. More and more, people interested in children—teachers, educators, doctors, Sunday school workers—have come to recognize that late childhood is not a dormant period, but a critical and exciting time of changing and growing, a time of stretching interests and awakenings of mind and spirit, a time of conflicts, tensions, and problems.

2. Nine Is a Turning-point Year

All people who have studied children agree that nine is one of the turning-point years in the growth cycle, a sort of divide or "watershed" year, a year that separates one part of life from another. Nine brings early childhood to a close and ushers in late childhood. One observer says that eight does not "turn into" nine, but "explodes" into nine. Junior is shifting gears into new territory, and we call that territory preadolescence. The term is meaningful to those who want to understand the drives and motives of the Junior child. He is next door to adolescence.

3. Juniors Are Subject to Conflicts and Problems

Some of the problems we have with Juniors grow out of their particular stage of growth. Junior has lived for a long time in a state of extreme dependence on adults, but the little time clock ticking away inside of him says it is time to untie the apron strings, to move out into a more self-directed life.

The trouble is, Junior does not have enough experience or information to function independently without making mistakes. This creates tension in his relationships with other children, with teachers, and with parents.

Something gets broken around a church and who is blamed? "Those Juniors!" A far-off noise shatters the peace of an adult meeting and someone whispers, "What are the Juniors up to now?" When asked to teach a Junior class, many adults decline with the excuse, "I am afraid I could not get them to behave."

No studies of Junior behavior in Sunday school have been made, but some studies have been made of their behavior in public school; and teachers of the fourth, fifth, and sixth grades report more behavior problems than teachers of any other grades. Children in these grades are nine, ten, and eleven.

When we hear the term "delinquent behavior," most of us are apt to think of teen-age boys and girls. Life with Juniors presents some large-scale problems, we teachers of nine-through-twelves say; but at least that thing, delinquency, need not shadow our thinking—not for a year or more.

The facts show that this thinking is wrong.

Students tell us that delinquency is far more apt to have its beginnings in Junior years than in adolescence. The fact that problem behavior more often expresses itself openly in adolescence has led people to identify this form of behavior with the teens, but those who know the facts look behind, back to late childhood and even earlier, to find the roots of the problems.

In its pamphlet, "Juvenile Delinquency," the U. S. Department of Health, Education, and Welfare, reports that in a study of 500 delinquent boys the fact was brought out that the age at which the largest number first appeared in court was between 11 and 13. Nine-tenths of these same children were having marked difficulty adjusting to normal social life before they were 11 years old—and almost a half of the group were giving noticeable signs of becoming delinquent at the age of 8 or younger. Delinquency begins early!

J. Edgar Hoover, director of the Federal Bureau of Investigation, U. S. Department of Justice, said in 1954: "Crime usually plants its seeds in the mind of a child during the early, formative years. It comes when there is a lack of something—lack of proper parental guidance, lack of wholesome companions, lack of discipline, lack of respect for the rights of others, disregard for parents and constituted authorities, the lack of emotional stability. The value of the church in filling many of these needs is obvious."

4. Juniors Are Ready for Christian Instruction

All the study of Juniors' behavior problems points toward a truth recognized by Junior workers ever since they have been studying Juniors—the Junior is at the peak of readiness for sound and basic Christian teaching.

Growing away from his former dependence on home and parents, identifying himself more and more with interests outside the home, mature enough to make choices for himself, the older child needs, more than anything else, a rock-sound motivation for choosing right instead of wrong, for thinking and acting in a way to develop the highest type of Christian manhood and womanhood.

What is the most trustworthy, the most durable motive we can offer children for right doing? Many motives have been tried and are tried every day, but only one is trustworthy—the fact that what they do *matters* to One who loved them enough to die to save them from wrongdoing—to save them in the hereafter—but also in the *here*.

Our Junior Sunday school work is centered on one basic belief: the Christian incentive is the best incentive for right acting.

5. Juniors Are Ready to Make a Decision for Christ

"How old were you when you became a Christian?" Over and over the writer has asked that question in groups of

Sunday school workers. And almost always the replies indicate that it was in the Junior period more than in any other that most people make their decisions to become followers of Jesus.

Why do more people accept Christ during Junior years than any other? The reason is found in the Junior himself, in his stage of growth. Those who live close to growing children know that usually in the Junior years there comes a new religious awakening, a heightened awareness of God that makes these years golden ones for evangelism.

The Junior is old enough to know that wrongdoing is a sin against God and to understand that Jesus came to earth and went to the cross to make a way for people out of their sin. He is old enough to know what it means to trust Jesus as his Saviour, old enough to understand what it means to pledge allegiance to Jesus and his way of life, old enough to study and work so that his own life may more and more harmonize with the pattern set by Jesus.

6. Juniors Are Changing in Their Attitudes

One fact noticed by all close observers of childhood is that Juniors are changing in three basic relationships—with adults, with other Juniors of their own sex, and with Juniors of the opposite sex.

These changes are well known to experienced Sunday school teachers. They have observed that Juniors do not defer to adult authority or "look up" to grownups as young children do; that in Junior years "the other boys" (in the case of boys) and "the other girls" (in the case of girls) exert a powerful influence on the Juniors' thinking and behaving—more powerful, it seems right now, than that of adults; they know that boy-girl antagonism is rampant, especially in the years nine through eleven.

(1) *Toward adults.*—Until he is about nine years old, the child's world revolves around the adults in his life, those who care for him, guide him, serve his needs. At first these are his parents; then, as his world expands, his teachers at school and at Sunday school.

One writer who has made a study of the development of children through the public-school years states that the outstanding positive relationship during the sixth, seventh, and eighth years is between the child and his teacher. The young child is too individualistic to be capable of satisfactory relationships with groups of other children. His play groups serve his own ends. Those who have tried team games with children under nine know how unsuccessful these efforts usually are.

But as a child grows toward nine, there is a gradual change of attitude. He begins to show a genuine interest in group life. He wants to be a part of a "gang" of his own sex and age. These gangs or groups seek one another's company, play together and often band themselves into a loose organization or "club."

It is from the other children now—not from adults—that the older child gets his strongest satisfactions.

This is hard for many adults to accept. One grandmother reported heartbrokenly that she had lost something precious in her life, the love of an adored granddaughter. Since babyhood Sally had spent Saturdays with her grandmother and now suddenly she chose to stay at home on Saturday and enjoy the companionship of the children in her neighborhood.

Of course this grandmother had not "lost" a granddaughter. Sally was responding to something deep, instinctive—the need for association with children her own age.

It was a healthy symptom of her nine-year-oldness.

Most adults are not too concerned because older children prefer the companionship of other children to their own. What does concern them is that Juniors seem to place more value on the approval of their "gang" or crowd than on that of adults. Mother may support with sound and logical arguments her case for Jimmy's wearing an overcoat instead of a sweater, but if the other boys scorn the overcoat, it is their verdict, not Mother's, that Jimmy accepts. Parents and teachers may insist on good English, but if the other boys say "ain't," Jimmy will speak as they do— away from home at least.

This fact—that older children are tremendously influenced by the standards and values of their own groups—greatly increases the reach of the Junior Sunday school teacher's responsibility. The teacher must do more than study Junior as an individual or as a member of his family; he must know something of the all-important gang with which this child spends most of his time—get some idea of their standards, their level of behaving and thinking. Many teachers visit the schoolrooms and the school playgrounds to study Juniors and their friends. Some let the pupils bring their friends to the class meetings and parties. This not only helps a teacher evaluate his pupils' friends, but it is often the means of bringing some of these boys and girls into the Sunday school.

And of course a teacher will always keep the door to his own classroom wide open to his pupils' friends on Sunday morning. He will welcome them and help them and make them feel needed and wanted and welcome.

(2) *Toward members of their own age and sex.*—The Junior's need to group together with children of his own age has been so generally recognized that the period has long been known as "the gang age." Recently another term, more dignified but carrying the same meaning, has come into use—the years of "co-ordinated group activity."

Juniors want to belong to a group of children—but not to *any* group of *any* children, they will thank you to remember. Juniors are rigidly insistent on two requirements. Their associates must be of their own sex and age. The latter requirement is almost as important as the first. Boys and girls only a little older seem as far away from Juniors as adults, separated as they are by the gulf of puberty; and children only a little younger are babies, they think. At no other age is the child so selective about his companions.

The typical Junior gang is small, consisting of about five or six members. In one study made of fifty-three groups of boys, no group had in it less than four or more than eight members. The gang is usually unstable in membership, has no stated purpose, rarely has a name.

The fact that these groups are called "gangs," does not imply that they are characterized by undesirable behavior. The gang may serve useful purposes—or it may be a factor contributing to delinquency. Boys who are unloved, rejected, unwanted, may use their gangs to strike back at the adult world which has misused them. One investigator recently traced his studies of delinquency invariably to the gang life of young boys in cities.

But under good conditions the group life of Juniors is a wholesome thing. Through their association with others, the boys and girls learn co-operation, develop wider interests, carry on common activities, and experience the discipline of give-and-take so necessary to a foundation for happy human relations. In fact, being accepted as a member of an age-group gang in Junior years seems a necessity for well-rounded growth.

(3) *Toward members of the other sex.*—There is one characteristic of younger Juniors about which all observers agree. Boys prefer the company of boys, and girls prefer the company of girls. We might make that statement stronger. In mid-Junior years (nine through eleven), most boys and girls seem actively to dislike each other.

Up through seven a child will choose a companion or a group of companions for play with no regard to sex. But sometime during eight there is a change. By nine the separation of the sexes for play and work is well under way, and by ten and eleven the boys and girls are completely segregated.

One study of children in their play life shows that sex differences in play interests are at a maximum from mid-eight to mid-ten.

But the Junior's choice of companions of his own sex is not confined to play. Studies have been made in schoolrooms to find whether Juniors prefer boys or girls as companions with whom to study. Starting in the fourth grade, about age nine, and lasting well into the eighth grade, age thirteen, it was found that boys choose boys and girls choose girls, almost to the complete exclusion of the opposite sex.

What are the reasons for the pulling apart of the sexes in Junior years? Several possible causes have been offered. Some say the antagonism is not real, but interest in the other sex camouflaged as antagonism. Some think it is the result of parents instilling into children almost from birth the difference in the way boys and girls should behave. Another possible cause is the earlier development of girls. The difference in growth between boys and girls begins early and continues well into adolescence. But the difference in growth rates is more pronounced in the years just preceding puberty, the Junior years. Not only are girls ahead of boys in physical growth, but they seem to develop earlier those skills which adults prize so highly. They speak and read with more ease, and they tend to conform more easily to adult patterns of behavior.

Girls at all ages through fifteen, have larger vocabularies than boys, but boys are ahead of girls in their ability to reason.

In a recent book *Growth and Development of the Preadolescent* by Blair and Burton, an interesting suggestion regarding grouping boys and girls for schoolwork is made. "Several possibilities suggest themselves as means of lessening the antagonism between the sexes at this level. One is that there seems to be more basis here than at any other level for classifying boys and girls separately in their school classwork. Some of the unfavorable comparisons might be eliminated. . . . Another possibility is that of avoiding the grouping of boys and girls within a class group for purposes of learning."[1]

This is an eye-opening comment, coming as it does out of a study of children's behavior in public school.

Because of the differences in boys' and girls' interests, because of their basic antagonism, because of the fact that girls are more mature in many ways than boys—it seems better to separate boys and girls for the class period.

---

[1]Blair and Burton, *Growth and Development of the Preadolescent* (New York: Appleton-Century-Crofts, Inc., 1951). Used by permission.

7. *Juniors Are Realists*

If he has a choice between a science story and a fairy story, Junior will choose the science story if he is over ten. He is apt to be more interested in *Popular Mechanics* magazine than in a children's magazine. Organized team games such as football and baseball are better games to Juniors than imaginary games like cowboys and Indians, Space Pilots, cops and robbers.

Junior is more impressed by what people do than by what they think and feel. Deeds on a bold, spectacular scale—those involving courage and loyalty—have more appeal for him than quiet deeds of kindness and generosity.

A Bible passage showing a person doing something can carry a truth over to a Junior better than an abstract passage. When a teacher talks of such generalized things as justice and charity and mercy, a Junior does not get much from the talk. But let the teacher share a story of a boy or girl who stood up for a wronged friend, or let him tell of people who share with a needy person, who showed these qualities in *deeds*—and the meanings of these vague terms will become clear.

All this is to say that the Junior is a realist, that he is more interested in what is true, what is actual, than in fantasy and imaginary deeds; that he is direct and forthright; that facts are important to him; that he appreciates tangible values rather than intangible ones; that he thinks concretely, not abstractly; that he is outgoing, not "inwardized" as the little child and the adolescent are apt to be.

These characteristics suggest why it is not wise to use symbolic teaching with Juniors. Symbolic teaching is an indirect route toward truth, and Juniors are direct in their approach to learning. Many of the object lessons, flannelgraph lessons, and chalk sermons prepared for children, while they attract interest through their novelty, fail entirely to do any teaching. Cords bound around a Junior's hands may represent the strangling effects of sin to his teacher—but to the Junior they are merely cords. Children cannot usually appreciate symbolic teaching until they are twelve or past twelve.

8. *Juniors Are Doers*

The need for almost constant physical activity is common to children of all ages. To say that excessive activity is a distinctive of or a characteristic peculiar to Juniorhood is not quite accurate. It *is* true that the range and variety of activities possible to Juniors are greater than those for younger children because of Juniors' improved motor coordination, more dependable balance, and greater stability in body proportions.

In Junior years, as in other years of childhood, there is an organic need for strenuous physical activity; bones and muscles are developing and require exercise. This should be remembered by those planning Sunday school rooms for Juniors. Cramped quarters and too-small, closed-in rooms prohibit freedom of movement—one cause of some of the problem behavior we sometimes have in Junior groups.

It is interesting for teachers to know that the years of relatively least growth in height are from nine to ten for girls and from ten to eleven for boys. Physically girls of eleven are a full year ahead of boys.

9. *Juniors Are Readers*

When a child can read, a whole new world of experience opens up to him. Most boys and girls can read and read well by the time they are nine. The old saying that Primary children are learning to read, but Juniors are reading to learn suggests a tremendous advantage that Junior Sunday school workers have. They can guide their Juniors in using their reading skills as a tool to find meanings in Bible passages. Juniors should have plenty of opportunity both in class and in assembly to search their Bibles meaningfully.

It is during Junior years that free reading, that is reading for pleasure, reaches its peak. Beginning at age nine, the amount of voluntary reading done by boys and girls increases steadily to about age thirteen, when it again usually drops off steadily. The reading level of the average adult—the amount of reading he does and the variety of his choices—is about equal to that of the typical eleven-year-old child.

Junior teachers can find out a great deal about Juniors by knowing what they read; then by reading the books themselves. Stories from good books may often be used to enrich teaching in class and in assembly.

10. *They Collect Things, Too*

The collecting urge reaches its peak between nine and eleven years of age. Boys and girls collect an amazing variety of objects. In one group of thirty Juniors queried by the writer, forty-four different objects were collected. They included shells, rocks, stamps, bent money, foreign money, baseball pictures, bottletops, match covers, church bulletins, bullets, and dolls.

Many a Sunday school teacher has found that the path to a Junior's heart leads right through his collecting hobby. He can show his interest in the collections, contribute to the collections, even, sometimes, use certain collected objects in the Sunday school.

II. How Shall We Find Out About Juniors?

Any man or woman who wants to know how best to provide for Juniors in his class or department must begin by taking a good long look at those Juniors, their needs, abilities, readinesses. There are two ways to do this, and teachers need to use both of them.

1. Find out everything possible about Juniors as a group.
2. Find out everything possible about each individual in the group.

1. *As an Age Group*

There are many ways a teacher may increase his knowledge of Juniors as a group.

Reading is one splendid opportunity. Fortunately, many

good books on child study are available. Titles may be found in the Junior section of the Baptist Book Store catalogues, in the book lists circulated by the Church Library Service, in leaflets devoted to Junior work, and in popular magazines.

Observing real, live Juniors is an even better way. Watch those Juniors on the playground. How have they grouped themselves for play? What kind of games are going on? Notice the ten-year-old on the bus seat across from you. Count the number of movements he makes in one ten-minute period. See those girls on the soda fountain stools? Listen to their conversation. Above all, use that special "mental hearing aid" that every teacher needs in order to pick up remarks Juniors make on Sunday morning; then ponder those remarks as you think about the Juniors.

2. *As Individuals*

Probably the best way for a teacher to gain an understanding of each individual is the simplest: just by being friends with him, visiting and talking with him personally.

Interviews with parents and visits in the home are indispensable. Observing the Junior in his playing—the way he reacts to other children, the way they react to him—adds immeasurably to the discerning teacher's mental photograph of the pupil. (See chap. 8 for detailed discussion of these techniques for studying Juniors.)

A Sunday school teacher can learn about a pupil by talking with previous Sunday school teachers. One word of caution: facts, not opinions, should be sought. But facts gathered through visiting and interviewing over a period of years are valuable and should be passed on to teachers seeking information about their pupils. It is as wasteful for a teacher to ignore facts compiled by another teacher as it would be for a doctor to refuse to look at a medical record of a patient compiled by another doctor.

One worker found out some useful information about Juniors' hobbies and play interests by preparing what she called "interest inventories," then asking the Juniors in her department to fill them out. Sheets were arranged so that Juniors could record, in the order of their preferences, such items as the type of books they read, the type of games they liked to play, the objects they collected. Here is a sample blank.

INTEREST INVENTORY

NAME _____ AGE _____

On the lines below write all the things you collect.

I like to collect _____ _____ _____

_____ _____ _____ _____

On the lines below write the games you like.

I like to play _____ _____ _____

_____ _____ _____ _____

Put a *1* by the kind of books you like best. Put a *2* by the kind of books you like next best, a *3* by those you like third best, a *4* by your fourth choice, and a *5* by your fifth choice.

___ Adventure stories
___ Stories of Bible heroes
___ Animal stories
___ Stories about real people
___ Comic books

III. WHAT ARE OUR PURPOSES FOR JUNIORS?

We have been looking at Juniors, studying their mental, physical, and spiritual qualities. Now we are ready to think about the question, "For what spiritual teachings are Juniors ready?" The answer to the question will be our purposes for Junior Sunday school work.

1. *Trusting Jesus as Lord and Saviour*

Our first purpose for Juniors in the Sunday school is to help them trust Jesus as their Lord and Saviour, to lead them to look to his living and his teaching as a pattern for their lives, to help them depend on his living presence—not just to "not do" things, but to *do*—to become a positive, constructive influence for good in all their relationships.

2. *Attending Church*

During Junior years we will try to help those Juniors who have trusted Jesus to become members of their church. We hope to help them become good stewards, to support their church with their presence in the meetings, their offerings, their interest, and their prayers. We will seek to lead Juniors to grow in the habit of regular church attendance—and of regular church *attention*, the habit, that is, of concentrating on and participating in each part of the order of worship.

3. *Learning from the Bible*

So much of our Junior Sunday school work centers around the Bible. Juniors' developed reading skills, increased attention span, and stretching horizons combine to make these four years an ideal time for orientation into Bible study. During Junior years boys and girls learn the names and groupings of the books of the Bible, get their first experiences in daily Bible readings and in using their Bibles in Sunday school, and memorize large portions of the Bible. During the years of these early Bible experiences we will help boys and girls to know that the Bible is God's Book, his revealed Word, the source of our knowledge of him—a Book given that we might know about his Son, that we might have a guide to right and wise living.

4. *Growing in Christian Living*

Conversion is just the beginning of the Christian life. After a person trusts Jesus as Lord and Saviour, he has Jesus' special help in living as a Christian—but he needs a lot of help in knowing what "living as a Christian" means. We need to give these young Christians Bible standards for conduct, to teach these standards plainly and positively; then guide the boys and girls in practicing Christian conduct in all their relationships every day.

Chapter 3

Grouping Juniors for Learning, Sharing, Worshiping

IN SEARCHING for the most helpful ways to group our Juniors, we must take into account not just those enrolled in Sunday school, but all the Juniors in the community who are not in any Sunday school. If these Juniors are in a family whose preference is for a Baptist church, or in a family that has no preference, they may be considered our Baptist possibilities. Certainly they should be taken into consideration in one important phase of grouping—determining the number of classes and departments necessary.

I. PLANNING FOR ALL—OUTSIDE JUNIORS, TOO

Basic to any good pattern for grouping boys and girls in Sunday school is the hope that the pattern may be outgrown as more Juniors are enrolled. To plan with a view to Juniors on the outside is more than sound Sunday school policy. It is Christianity spelled out in planning. It is sharing with Jesus a feeling about people, for when he talked of fields white unto harvest and a sheep separated from his shepherd, Jesus was speaking of *people*, of boys and girls, men and women, in need of the very thing that those cut off from Sunday school are in need of—the chance to know that God loves them and wants them—that he has a plan to save and change them.

1. Many Juniors Are Unreached

Many Junior workers tend to be complacent about their responsibility for Juniors on the outside of Sunday school.

They say—and believe—that they are reaching most of the Junior possibilities. Those large numbers of unreached people they hear about are Intermediates, young people, adults, but not Juniors. *Or so they think.*

What are the facts? While it is true that, as a rule, census returns show fewer prospects for the Junior group than for any other age group, our Southern Baptist churches are reaching less than half of their Junior possibilities. At this writing (1955) the Southern Baptist handbook lists the number of boys and girls of Junior age in our territory at approximately 5,198,378. Of this number, 877,196 are enrolled in Southern Baptist Sunday schools. But there are 1,906,472 Juniors not being reached by any Sunday school!

2. *It Costs to Neglect Them*

The thought of two million Juniors missing out on all the important learnings they are so ready for in Junior years is enough to turn any worker's mind and heart away from the *four* corners of his Sunday school room to the *far* corners of his community. If a boy or girl grows out of Juniorhood without the spiritual experiences these years make him ripe for—commitment to Christ, induction into Bible study, growth of stewardship habits—he will never completely make up for this lack, even if he accepts Christ and learns the way of Christian living in later years. Just as right development of bones and muscles and tissue depends on good nutrition while these parts of the body are in the growing stage, so fine and balanced Christian character depends on early acceptance of Christ and day-by-day experiences in Christian living, experiences that keep pace with the individual's developing understandings and abilities.

Christ can save and change a person at any stage of life, but the person who waits must pay for the wasted years. Conservation of boys and girls is so much less costly than reclamation of men and women. The slogan of a boys' club—"Better to Build Boys Than to Mend Men"—reminds us of the peculiar responsibility that rests on workers with boys and girls in the Sunday school.

3. *Juniors Can Be Located*

Where shall we look to find the Juniors who are out of Sunday school? There are some Junior prospects everywhere, but the great majority of the unenlisted Juniors are away from the reach of the older, more established churches. Some of these Juniors are in rural sections, some are in new centers of population—growing residential developments, industrial centers, newly developed housing projects, underprivileged sections of great cities. The most practical way a Junior worker can help the Juniors in the underchurched areas is to join with other members of the church to start a branch Sunday school there. The movement to take churches to the people when the people do not take to the churches has grown rapidly among Southern Baptists in the last few years, and has been a dynamic force in reaching Juniors on the fringes of our church communities.

But there are always some unreached Juniors within the radius of every church. We find them in families of newcomers to town, in the schoolrooms, on the rolls of Vacation Bible schools, and nearly always on the returns from a church census.

4. *Everybody's Business—Finding Juniors*

Juniors can and should be enlisted in finding the unreached Juniors. It is a practical and right-at-hand opportunity to put missionary lessons into action. The efforts of the Juniors, however, cannot substitute for those of teachers and officers. Sometimes it takes the combined work of teacher, superintendent, associate and Juniors, too, to find, enlist, then anchor a Junior prospect to the Sunday school. Many a "found" Junior has become a "lost" Junior—lost, that is, to the Sunday school because a Junior worker gave up after one visit into the home.

II. FINDING HELPFUL WAYS OF GROUPING

When we know our possibilities, when we have counted and studied the Juniors in our midst, then we are ready to decide on a plan of grouping that fits the Junior and contributes to the long-range purposes of the Sunday school. Three factors guide us.

1. *The Age of the Junior*

Our studies in chapter two showed us that certain characteristics and abilities are common to most children of a given age. It seems best, then, to group our Juniors first on the age basis. The age range should be kept as narrow as the number of Juniors will allow.

Grouping by age means, first of all, putting all the nine-, ten-, and eleven-, and twelve-year boys and girls into the group called the Juniors. To put Juniors with Primary or Intermediate groups—even when there are only two or three Juniors—is to deny them opportunity to reach their maximum spiritual stature during these years.

Within the four-year span there should be classes for each age, and as enrolment grows, workers should plan toward a department for each age. A teacher with nine-year-olds only in his class has a much better opportunity to relate his Bible teaching to nine-year-old living, and a superintendent with nine-year-olds only in his department can greatly strengthen his period if all are studying one lesson, memorizing one Bible passage, and working toward the same unit purposes.

2. *The Sex of the Junior*

We noticed in chapter 2 that many differences in boys and girls begin to show up in Junior years, that their reading tastes, collecting hobbies, and play interests start taking different directions late in the eighth and early in the ninth year. We found, too, that physically girls develop earlier than boys, and that in Junior years more than in any other years, the mental abilities of boys and girls express themselves in different ways, girls usually excelling in verbal skills, and boys in subjects involving reasoning powers.

So it seems more efficient from every standpoint to group Juniors by sex for the Bible study period, putting girls in girls' classes, and boys in boys' classes. This Bible study period is the only period for which they should be divided, however. They should be together in all department-wide activities. It is never wise to have a boys' department and a girls' department, nor is it good practice to have separate department socials for boys and girls. All we do for boys and girls while they are growing up should make it easy, not hard, for them to stand together as men and women—to bring about Christ's purposes in this world together. To that end we should help them have experiences right now in planning, sharing, learning together.

But for the class period we separate boys and girls. That is because these Bible lessons are fitted to the shape of life, and, as we have seen, life is beginning to be different for boys and girls by Junior time. Always it is easier to guide the learning of a group if it is together in its interests and abilities. This is especially true when time for teaching is limited. When a teacher has only girls in her class, she can begin her lesson in a way more interesting to girls, can enrich it with activities more in line with girls' interests, and apply it in more practical, down-to-earth ways. The same is true when a teacher has only boys in his class.

Men teachers for boys.—There are many reasons why it is better for men to teach boys and women to teach girls. Men know the problems boys face and women know the problems girls face—know them from the best of all possible sources—firsthand experience.

Certainly men can minister to the social life of boys more satisfactorily than women can. They can organize ball teams; can take the boys on hikes, trips, cookouts. Men can speak a boy's language, can provide the adult masculine companionship that growing boys need.

But most of all, men are teaching boys something just by being in Sunday school with them Sunday after Sunday. It is a vivid, forceful lesson, one without words: "Sunday school is important for men, too; just as important as it is for women and children."

Boys need to know that you don't outgrow the necessity for Sunday school when you outgrow childhood.

3. *The Number of Juniors*

There should be a class for *at least* every nine Junior possibilities. A class for six or seven Junior possibilities is much more satisfactory. If there are as many as five or six Junior possibilities in a Sunday school, there should be two classes, one for boys and one for girls. These two classes may meet separately for Sunday morning classwork and even an assembly period.

If there are as many as 25 Junior possibilities, there should be four classes, nine- and ten-year boys in one, and eleven- and twelve-year boys in another; and girls, of course, grouped similarly. A fully organized department is desirable in this case. When there are 50 Juniors, there can be a fully graded department, a class for each age and sex. When the enrolment of a department comes to 75 to 80, there should be two departments with nine- and ten-year-olds in one department and eleven- and twelve-year-olds in another. When enrolment reaches 150 Juniors, there may be four departments, one for each age.

A dividing line.—Grading by age necessitates a dividing line for classifying pupils. The first of April is the date usually used. If the first of April is used, a pupil who will be ten years old by March 31 will be classified as a ten-year-old on Promotion Day. *There is a decided advantage in using April 1 as the dividing line.* It makes it possible for Juniors to be promoted to the Intermediate department at a younger age. If January 1 is used as the dividing line, a Junior whose birthday is in January will be nearly fourteen when he is promoted from the Junior department—and this sometimes leads to restlessness and dissatisfaction.

In small units—Junior classes and departments should be kept small for many reasons. Small units are better for *teaching*, better for *reaching*. When a teacher has six Juniors on roll, he has more incentive to seek new members. In a small class, a teacher can teach informally, allowing pupils to learn by doing, thinking, talking, asking, discussing, writing, exploring, searching, and reading. In a large class, the teacher must do most of the talking, while the pupils' activity is limited to listening.

With a small class, a teacher can know each pupil as an individual. With twenty Juniors on roll, the teacher has a "class"; with seven on roll he has a little group of friends, each one a well-known and well-loved personality.

Nine-year-old Sue was beaming when she came home from Sunday school one day. "The nicest thing happened today," she told her mother. "Lots of children were absent, and Miss Graham smiled at me. It was a smile just for me, not for everybody. I guess," she said wistfully, "when you have so many in the class, it takes a long time to get around to smiling at everybody."

When a Junior just has one fifteenth or one twelfth of a teacher, that Junior is being cheated out of a basic right— the right to a good-sized portion of his teacher's time and attention and concern and interest.

With a small enrolment a teacher can extend Sunday school into the week. He can visit, keep up with absentees (and "presentees"), recognize birthdays, write friendly notes and cards, report to parents, and engage in the many, many gestures that nurture friendship between a teacher and a pupil.

Having a small enrolment in the department benefits the superintendent in similar ways. The superintendent should be able to greet each Junior personally, to call his name in the assembly. It is an admission of failure when a superintendent must call a Junior, "the boy in the blue shirt," or "the girl on the back seat."

Also having a small department with fewer classes and teachers cuts down on the superintendent's administrative responsibilities and frees him for more creative tasks.

III. HELPING JUNIORS GROW THROUGH SHARED RESPONSIBILITIES

Not only do Juniors like to do things, they like some freedom in doing these things "on their own," without the too-close supervision of adults. The urge for more independence in making choices, in planning and carrying through a piece of work, is right and normal for Juniors, and should be respected. In order to become self-directed adults, boys and girls must have experiences that build self-reliance while they are boys and girls.

1. *Juniors Can Assume Responsibilities*

As we shall see in a later chapter, teachers have opportunities on Sunday morning for guiding Juniors in working alone and in groups, but they should also allow the Juniors to plan and carry on some of the work of the class—and even that of the department. Juniors can work to build up attendance; they can find prospects for the class and bring them in; they can create interest in church attendance, lesson study, and memorization of passages; they can keep the room clean and tidy, plan socials, take care of materials, gather class news for the department news journal, counsel with the superintendent in planning programs, and in many other ways make worth-while contributions to the total work of the Junior group.

2. *Several Plans Are Possible*

There are several possible plans for grouping Juniors within the class to carry out activities. We shall consider the three most workable plans.

(1) *Informal committees.*—Under this plan the various tasks of the class are entrusted to special chairmen. This chairman retains his office for three months (the time may be longer), but he may work with any number of the other Juniors as the job requires. Sometimes he needs several helpers; sometimes he can handle his job alone.

The missionary chairman is responsible for keeping up class interest in finding and enlisting new members, and for keeping regular members attending each Sunday. He may telephone, write, and visit absentees. He develops his "seeing-eye" powers to find Juniors not in Sunday school, and to help the other members to become prospect-minded. This "missionary" may introduce new members and visitors in the assembly. He may give quarterlies to new members. He may enter the names of new Christians in the department Bible. He may work to get Juniors to attend Training Union.

The church attendance chairman works to get each class member to attend preaching services. He does this first by setting the example himself. He may find out the pastor's sermon topic and tell the class about it; he may report to the associate superintendent the number of class members attending that month. He may work with others in preparing a chart or graph showing progress of church attendance. He may accept the Standard of Excellence certificate from the superintendent and hang it in his classroom.

The Bible study chairman is responsible for creating interest in all phases of Bible study—in preparing the weekly lesson, in memorizing the memory verse and Bible passages. He may report to the associate in charge of memory work the number from his class who have memorized their memory passages and hymns.

Many times the teacher enriches the memorizing of a Bible passage by a piece of creative handwork, such as booklets, friezes, posters. To secure necessary supplies for such activities is the responsibility of the Bible study chairman.

The room chairman keeps the room neat and orderly. He has charge of taking supplies from the cabinet on Sunday morning and returning them. He keeps chalkboard clean and supplied with chalk and eraser. He keeps notices on class bulletin board up to date. He helps in room exhibits, for example, a Bible exhibit, a nature or a missionary center.

The meetings chairman works with the teacher to find a place for the class meetings. He may contact the various parents. He plans games and refreshments with the help of teacher and pupils.

The letter and telephone chairman has a list of addresses and telephone numbers of all the class. He calls about special days and offerings. He writes necessary letters—to the parents in whose homes the class meets, to sick persons in the class or church. He encourages the writing of notes and cards to Juniors who are on vacation. The teacher can contact this chairman when he has class telephoning to do and enlist his help in getting other Juniors to help him.

The news chairman gathers news for the department newspaper or news sheet, which many Junior groups mimeograph, circulate among the Juniors, and send into the homes for the parents to read. If no news sheet is circulated, the news chairman may gather items for announcements in assembly—items such as names of sick, absentees who have returned, socials, meetings, outings, names of new Christians, and so on.

Other helpers.—Many teachers will think of other tasks that they might assign to the Juniors. A job should be assigned to every Junior, so the above outline should be elastic and flexible.

One teacher's plan.—Here is the way one teacher guided her class in deciding on and choosing responsibilities under the preceding plan. After gathering the girls together, she suggested that they make a list of the jobs that needed to be done to maintain a good working class. "Somebody ought to keep our table clean," volunteered Judy. "And clean the chalkboard so it will be nice for Training Union," another suggested. The teacher wrote down both suggestions. "A lot of us aren't 100 per cent," said Thelma, "Somebody ought to be working on that." So another suggestion was listed. Other suggestions included: "Taking care of maps and pictures," "Finding and bringing Juniors not in Sunday school," "Helping Mrs. R. with plans for parties," "Gathering class news." All these suggestions were written down.

The next step was to go through the list and group together jobs that were closely related. For example, it was decided that the task of cleaning board, straightening table, and looking after supplies belonged together and could be taken over by the same person. In thinking through the job of "helping everybody be 100 per cent," the teacher led pupils to name the only points on which they were falling down—attending preaching services and studying lessons. Obviously these were the only points that the Juniors needed to work on.

Next the teacher and the Juniors suggested names for the Juniors who might assume jobs—"Room chairman," "Missionary chairman," and so on. Since the class included only four pupils, some jobs had to include many and varied duties.

Then the teacher asked the group to decide who should do which job. "I think Judy ought to work on lesson study and preaching attendance," said one, "because she is always 100 per cent." Everybody agreed that this was fair. Others were chosen in the same way, and everybody felt satisfied.

(2) *Class officers.*—Another plan that has long been in use in Junior groups is that of the organized class. Under this plan the class members meet together with the teacher on a weekday and elect a president, vice-president, and secretary. Committees are formed and other Juniors elected as chairmen. This plan of organization can work very well with older Juniors, but many workers have found it not suited to the limited abilities of nine-year-olds. For that reason the plan just outlined is suggested as a possibility with younger groups.

After presenting the plan of organization and explaining the duties of the officers, the teacher should receive nominations. The vote may be by ballot or by the raising of hands. Since all pupils like to hold office, it is well to elect the class officers each quarter. An officer may be re-elected any time during the year.

The teacher should see that each officer understands his duties. It is effective to have the officers stand and state their duties; then pledge to carry them out faithfully.

The class should select a scheme, including name, colors, aim, Scripture verse, and song. The class may select one of the schemes suggested in this leaflet, for which pennants and pins are available, or they may make one of their own.

If the pupils wish, they may adopt the name and scheme of the class to which they have been promoted. This is the custom in some schools.

(3) *Spontaneous groupings as needs arise.*—Still another idea is to allow the Juniors to group into committees as the needs arise. Under this plan, officers or chairmen will be formally elected, but assignment of duties will grow out of natural situations. For example, if a Bible exhibit is being

planned to culminate a unit on "How We Got Our Bible," the teacher and Juniors would make a list of things that need to be done; then they would decide on committees. The Juniors would choose the committees on which they would wish to serve.

This plan can be followed in planning a party, in planning to give a food gift to a needy family, in planning to dramatize a Bible story for the assembly, and in many other instances.

3. Class Meetings Are Important

A Junior class should hold a weekday meeting at least once a month. The meeting may take place at the church, at the home of a teacher, or in the homes of the Juniors. Meeting in the homes of pupils is especially desirable, for it serves to enlist the interest of the parents and make them contributors to class activities. This is a good way to strengthen parent-teacher relationships (see chap. 9).

Class meetings serve many useful purposes. They stimulate a spirit of friendliness and togetherness on the part of the Juniors. They provide opportunities to practice the teachings of the lessons. They give the teacher a chance to see his pupils in a more natural situation, to observe how they adjust to other boys and girls, how they accept defeat or victory in a game. They are one fine way to extend the Sunday school ministry into the week.

Class meetings are a way to stretch the all-too-few Sunday morning minutes. In the meetings the Juniors with their teacher may work on creative projects—illustrating memory work passages, making posters, working on gifts or cards for others. One girls' group met in the home of the teacher to make Easter cards for shut-ins. Another made gifts for the ladies in a home for the aged and tray cards for a hospital. Another worked on a wall picture, and one class made valentines for the superintendent whose birthday was in February. Making Promotion Day badges for the new Juniors or corsages for the graduating Juniors is another idea.

Older Juniors may have more formal meetings with president presiding, and secretary reading the minutes; but for younger Juniors, an informal meeting is more in line with their abilities.

The class meeting is a good time to study the records and to make plans for improving in Bible study and lesson study, and in church attendance.

Fun and food should always have a place in the class meeting.

Class names and schemes get interest.—No matter how the Juniors group to carry on the work of the class, they can enjoy choosing a name, colors, verse, aim, and song. These may be original or they may be chosen from those prepared by the Department of Junior Sunday School Work, Baptist Sunday School Board at Nashville 3, Tennessee. Workers may write this department for information.

Chapter 4

The Right Workers for Juniors

So MANY Sunday schools cannot provide what they know is right and good for their Juniors. Their space is limited, their equipment inadequate, their buildings anything but ideal. But there is one thing that need never be limited or inadequate or less than ideal—one resource that any church anywhere can provide richly for its children. The *human* material, the men and women who work with the Juniors on Sunday, can always be of first quality. When that is true, when the workers are dedicated and understanding and conscientious, no other lack can seriously hurt the work. If the workers are untrained and unfit, the finest buildings, the most expensive equipment will profit a school nothing.

I. What Kind of Workers Are Needed?

The worker himself, then, is the most important factor in the network of factors that make up Sunday school organization. "Not all the books on all the shelves, but what the workers are themselves—" that is what counts.

The reason for this gets us down to a bedrock truth about teaching in the Sunday school. Teaching (and every worker who shares in the Sunday morning program is a teacher) is primarily a matter of sharing. Someone has even defined teaching as "the sharing of truth through means of personality for eternal ends." A lesson comes to the pupil *through the teacher*. Joseph or Paul or the boy Timothy may have been the central figure in last Sunday's lesson—but the teacher who taught it was in the lesson, too. His beliefs, his convictions, his thinking colored all he said and did—and all the pupils learned. It was this principle Paul had in mind when he wrote to the Christians at Corinth: "Ye are . . . the epistle of Christ . . . written not with ink, but with the Spirit of the living God; not in tables of stone, but in fleshy tables of the heart" (2 Cor. 3:3). Teachers are *living* lessons. Not all Juniors study Sunday school lessons, but all study Sunday school teachers. Not all Juniors read the Bible—but all Juniors read teachers.

1. *Workers Who Are Spiritually Adequate*

Sunday school is a spiritual business—so the first requirement concerns the worker's spiritual adequacy. What do we mean by spiritual adequacy?

(1) *Workers who have accepted Christ.*—This is an essential for any worker anywhere in the Sunday school, but for one who works with boys and girls in the crucial, choice-making Junior years, the requirement has a special urgency. A person who has never had the experience of trusting Jesus as Saviour can hardly lead another to trust him. A worker with Juniors must be one who, at some time in his life, has faced and made a choice—the choice to take Jesus as his Saviour, to turn around in his living until he faces in the same direction with Jesus, to try, with Jesus' help to go in his direction from now on. A Christian is not just someone who is trying to live as Jesus lived—period. A Christian is someone who is trying to live as Jesus lived *because*—and the words that follow are the important ones—because a thing has happened to him, a heart-changing, life-transforming thing we call conversion.

(2) *Church members.*—Joining the church will not save a person, but it is hard to imagine a saved person who does not join a church. A person who works with Juniors should be not only a church member, but a member of the church in which he is teaching. This is a matter of simple honesty. The whole Junior team is trying to help each Junior become a member of the church after he has committed his heart and life to Jesus. A worker who has not taken the step certainly cannot speak with conviction on the subject. He can even *undo* much positive teaching done by others.

(3) *Those who cultivate the spiritual life.*—It comes as a

surprise to some people that the Christian life has to be delib-
erately cultivated—that the soul depends on certain foods for
its vigor and well-being as does the body.

Praying is one of these foods. This means true praying, for
if prayer is to nourish the spirit, it must be more than the saying of words or the repeating of forms or the requesting of
things. As its highest and best, praying is sharing with God,
thinking toward God, tuning into God—into his power and
energy and creativeness so that a little bit of that power and
creativeness and energy gets into us.

A Junior worker needs to pray for so many things—for his
pupils, for his purposes, for light on his problems, for wisdom
to know God's will. But mostly he just needs to pray. Next to
bringing a child into the world, the most creative job in the
world is the job of helping a child grow *toward* Christ, then
leading him to Christ. No human being has enough creative
power to do that alone. He must have a partner, one who will
share some of his own creative energy. A teacher needs to
pray.

Daily Bible *using* is another vitamin that nourishes the
spiritual life. Notice the word "use." That means more than
Bible reading. To use the Bible means to study it, search it,
explore it, test it by practical experience. I heard of an elderly
Christian who spent a long lifetime in that last-named practice. After his death relatives, looking through his worn and
marked Bible, noticed on almost every page the initials *T* and
P. The verses marked had been "tried" and "proved." The old
Christian had seen these truths work out in his own experience, had learned through life itself that the Bible *works*.
That is true Bible *using*.

Practicing Christian living is another spiritual vitamin. A
person becomes a Christian in a very short moment—in the
moment it takes to recognize that Christ is his Saviour, and to
commit his life to him. But becoming *Christian* requires a
long lifetime of seeking and striving and growing and trying
again, even after discouraging failures.

A Junior worker, whose life is dedicated to helping new
Christians take their first steps as Christians, needs to study

every word Jesus spoke, every act recorded in the Gospels until he gets inside the mind and thinking of Jesus. When he does, he is able to glimpse something of the breadth and height and depth of the ideal Jesus blueprinted for us in his Gospels. Being Christian goes far beyond a "not-do" program. Naturally a Christian will try to avoid the major sins, but to stop there is not even to touch the fringe of Christian thinking. Being Christian goes far beyond doing "things"—even right and necessary things like going to church, reading the Bible, and giving the tithe. Being Christian means doing these things and much more. It means getting into our thinking and our doing those values Jesus stressed over and over —humility, forgiveness, willingness to repay wrong with kindness, love, mercy, and respect for human personality, all human personality wherever and whoever it is.

2. Workers Who Are Sympathetic with Problems of Juniors

Is childhood a carefree, trouble-free time—all sunshine and cloudless skies? Think back to your childhood and you will not even ask. Boys and girls have troubles. They have problems that baffle and bewilder and hurt. How to get along in school, how to measure up to what parents expect and what the gang demands, worrying about being rejected by other children, worrying about family finances, worrying over wrong things they have done—these are some of the problems common to most Juniors. Then there are special problems that come to special children—the breakup of a home, the illness of a parent, the remarriage of a parent, the enforced separation from a mother who has recently gone to work.

Some children have troubles like the particular trouble that happened to Joe. Because Joe's father was well in his body, it was a long time before anybody realized that he was sick in his mind. Joe watched while the father he had known and loved turned into a stranger—hostile, suspicious, someone to be feared—and his ten-year-old world caved in. But Joe's Sunday school teacher found out, and during the terrible months before his father was taken to an institution, the teacher tried to be a father to him, taking him on trips with his own sons, inviting him to his home.

A good teacher will *know*. A good teacher will care and help. He will do what everybody must do if he is to help another—learn to step over to the other person's side, try to see how things look from there. A missionary to Africa once said, "I was never able to help those people of Africa—really help —until I learned to *think African*." A good teacher will *think Junior*, will be interested in the problems the Juniors have, because he is interested supremely in the Junior behind the problem.

3. *Workers Who Continue to Grow*

Because a Junior's mind is so alive, so eager in its push and strain after new understandings, those who work with Juniors must be alive in their minds, too. A person who is not healthily interested in adding to his store of knowledge and wisdom will never be vital enough in his leadership and secure enough in his teaching to challenge Juniors.

Good teachers teach out of an overflow of knowledge. They have in their minds and hearts far more than they give out in their teaching. A teacher who relies on past learnings rather than continually adding to his knowledge will soon wear thin. His teaching will reflect his meager resources. Paul highlighted this truth in his word to the Romans, "Thou . . . that teachest another, teachest thou not thyself?" (Rom. 2:21 ASV).

A Junior worker should constantly study—study his Bible, study children, study the world. He should listen—listen to parents, to other teachers, to boys and girls. He should observe, discuss, evaluate, ponder. He should think. He should keep abreast of the surge and swell of happenings everywhere in his town, his denomination—in the world of religion and the whole exciting, changing world he lives in. "The hearing ear, and the seeing eye, the Lord hath made even both of them" (Prov. 20:12). And the teacher should use even both of them, use them to enrich his mind, nourish his spirit, stretch his vision.

4. *Workers Who Are Dependable and Responsible*

A superintendent said of a teacher, "I am afraid she is not teaching those Juniors very much. She is irresponsible."

But an irresponsible teacher *is* teaching. She is teaching by her negative example—teaching that Sunday school is not very important ("She comes in late every Sunday."); teaching that religion is for Sunday only ("She never calls us during the week."); teaching that Sunday school is a place where you sit around and do nothing ("She studies her lesson in the early time while we just sit there with nothing to do.")

Sometimes a teacher who does not measure up is not actually irresponsible. Some new teachers do not understand the importance of visiting every pupil; do not see why they should attend the weekly workers' meeting; do not know how to use the important early minutes on Sunday morning. Helping teachers understand and meet the requirements of their job is one of the responsibilities of the superintendent. Every new teacher should be acquainted with certain minimum requirements:

1. Be at Sunday school at least 15 minutes ahead of time
2. Attend weekly workers' meeting
3. Visit adequately
4. Prepare the lesson adequately
5. Be present every Sunday unless providentially hindered

II. Where Will We Find the Workers?

There is no quick, easy answer. As in all matters pertaining to Sunday school work, the key to the problem lies in people, in the vision and imagination and resourcefulness of the men and women who do the looking for and enlisting of workers. Since there are seldom any trained, diploma-holding teachers sitting idly around churches waiting to be asked to take Junior classes, the task of finding workers calls for a special kind of insight—the art of seeing promise in the unpromising, the ability to look at people as they are and see deep down the teachers they might become.

Finding the right teachers is the most difficult part of a leader's work—and the most rewarding. It is the highest challenge to his leadership. Now, where will we find the workers?

1. *Church Members Not Working in Sunday School*

Yes, there are such people in every church—Christians who ought to be working and who will work if found and challenged and encouraged and trained. Sometimes they do not look like teachers—like our own mental picture of teachers— so we ignore them, allow them to sit around our churches wasting their talents year after year.

Dr. Sands was one of these "lost" church members. For three years he had sat in a pew and a class—unused and unhappy. Then a Junior superintendent who had eyes to see enlisted him as a Junior teacher. Said Dr. Sands, when he accepted the class, "I had made up my mind to move my membership this year. I was going to some church that would put me to work." Today this young dentist is superintendent of the department in which he was enlisted not so long ago as an inexperienced teacher.

Looking over groups of members assembled in all church meetings is a rewarding exercise. Faces leap out—nice, honest faces that twinkle with good humor—and an alert superintendent makes a mental note, "That face should belong to a teacher of Juniors."

Searching the church roll is another profitable practice. When a superintendent looks over the names of members of his church, when he searches *believing*, searches *praying*, his faith is nearly always rewarded. Some name steps off the roll, a name that somehow he had missed before.

The difficulty in securing workers is usually not lack of prospects, but lack of belief in people. We find a prospect; then we ourselves supply him with imaginary excuses: "He is such a busy man. He could not possibly teach." But has not the Lord's work always been done by busy people? Remember what Matthew was doing when Jesus called him? What Peter was doing—and Andrew and James and John?

Or we say, "She is too timid; she would not possibly"—forgetting that building up self-confidence in those who feel inadequate, inspiring the uninspired, is one of the responsibilities of leadership.

2. New Church Members

Happily most Baptist churches are healthily growing. Among the new members coming into churches, we find a good source of prospective teachers. Many of these have had experience with Juniors, and many others can, with some training, become good teachers. A superintendent will want to keep a list of all new members and after consulting with the proper persons—general superintendent, or director of education, or a committee composed of these and others—get permission to interview certain ones about becoming Junior workers.

3. Vacation Bible School Faculty

The Vacation Bible school is certainly not a mere proving ground for Sunday school teachers. Nevertheless, many fine workers volunteer to help in the short season of Vacation Bible school when they would not accept the responsibility of a full-time class. Such workers, once interested in the boys and girls, are often willing to continue their work through the Sunday school. In Vacation Bible school teachers prove their ability—or lack of it. For these and other reasons, Junior Sunday school workers should keep in close touch with the work of the Vacation Bible school.

4. Parents of Juniors

Parents have a valuable investment in the Sunday school— their own children. Any fair-minded mother and father will recognize the debt they owe the Sunday school, and feel some responsibility for contributing to a work that has contributed so much to them. There is another reason why parents can often be enlisted as workers. They are interested in every influence touching their children. They like to know and to know first-hand what the Sunday school is doing and how their children are responding. A thoughtful superintendent will study the talents of parents and try to use them wisely and effectively.

5. *Adult Classes and Training Union*

The teacher of an Adult class or the leader of an Adult union is in position to give Junior teachers invaluable assistance. Not only can an Adult teacher supply names of prospective teachers, but he can advise with regard to their dependability and their ability. A Junior superintendent should keep in close touch with these Adult leaders. Because they know the adult life of the church so well, they can often advise about any teacher under consideration—even those who are not in their classes.

A good Adult teacher will consider this a part of his own work, for his ability to turn inactive adults into active functioning workers throughout the church is one proof of his vigor and effectiveness as a teacher.

III. How Shall We Enlist Them?

Here is another question to which there can be no quick and easy answer. To enlist workers successfully calls for all those qualities that make for success in human relations—tact, consideration, understanding, courtesy, sympathetic insight, respect for another's feelings. It calls for something else—the ability to communicate one's own feelings to another—one's sense of the bigness of this job, the urgency of the need, one's own infectious enthusiasm for its boundless opportunities.

There are also some broad principles to remember, principles which, if understood and followed, will make successful enlisting of workers more possible and more enjoyable.

1. *Pray the Lord of the Harvest*

The first thing to do when faced with the problem of many, many Juniors and few, few teachers is to give Jesus' plan a try. "The Juniors truly are plenteous," Jesus might have been saying in the words recorded in Matthew 9:37, "but the teachers are few." And his plan for meeting the emergency? "Pray ye therefore the Lord of the harvest...."

Isn't it strange how many superintendents, concerned as they are, neglect to enlist the help of One even more concerned about the harvest? "I am not working at this problem alone," a superintendent should remember. "God cares, too. I will ask him to be my partner; then there will be two of us working together at this job."

Prayer changes things—even worker shortages. For so often, as we pray, we find ourselves recalling someone else who might be asked—or someone who might be asked *again*. And always our will-to-do, our own ingeniousness and resourcefulness are deepened as we talk with and listen to God.

2. *Convey a Vision*

The ultimate goal in successful enlistment is more than getting someone to take the job. It is getting him to *want* to take it. Begging a prospect to take a class, asking him to do this thing "as a personal favor," understating the extent of the work involved—these approaches will lead to failure in the long run, even if they do get an immediate commitment. One of our fine Sunday school leaders likes to say: "I never beg anybody to take a class. I just beg him to pray about taking a class." Sometimes it is possible to challenge a prospective teacher by giving him a list of the names of a class and asking him to pray for those Juniors. It sometimes helps to invite him to the department on Sunday morning and let him meet and talk with the Juniors.

3. *Hold Up High Standards*

A certain good superintendent, when asked how she managed to enlist and keep so many good teachers, replied, "When I enlist a worker, I make the job sound hard." Is it not human nature to respond more readily to the challenge of a big task than to that of a small one? When we are asked by someone who has high standards to take a certain job, our respect for the job and our respect for ourselves is increased.

Holding up high standards is a way to screen out undesirable workers. Playing down the work involved may attract some people, but not the stable, worth-while, enduring type of worker we want for our Juniors. It saves time to state honestly the scope of the work involved in taking a class—the amount of visiting that is expected, the responsibility to support the weekly meeting, the amount of preparing necessary to teach a good lesson.

4. Develop the Far Look

This means to look ahead, to have a long-range program of worker-enlistment. It is a short-sighted superintendent who waits until he has a resignation to look for a worker. "I would no more be without a few teachers in reserve than I would live up to the limit of my income," said a good superintendent —one who has a fine record of securing and holding workers. The superintendent who has one or two workers in reserve, who keeps a weather-eye on the possibilities in his church, is not helpless when a teacher suddenly resigns; he does not have to combine classes or teach a class himself when an emergency arises.

Taking the far look means "talking Juniors" with the people of the church; singling out a promising young man or woman in the Young People's department, someone perhaps the Juniors like, and talking Juniors to him; handing him helpful material to read; getting him (or her) Junior-minded against the day when he will be ready to take a class.

Two words have come recently into our vocabulary—"remedial" and "preventive." In medicine we know what they mean, and we know that preventive effort is more sensible and more economical than remedial efforts.

It is more sensible in this matter of teacher enlistment, too. A superintendent who helps his teachers stay happy, who guides them toward success in their work, who counsels with them in moments of discouragement, who commends good work where it is merited, that superintendent is preventing resignations and saving himself unnecessary work.

5. Live with the Problem

That is the secret—to live with the problem, to breathe it, to think it, to pray it. A teacherless class should haunt the superintendent, not just as Sunday approaches but on all days—at the circle meeting on Monday afternoon or at the Brotherhood meeting on Monday night, at the market on Tuesday. When a superintendent "thinks Junior teachers" constantly, he will find Junior teachers.

IV. How Shall We Train the Workers?

When he has enlisted a worker, the superintendent's work has only begun. In many cases the enlistee lacks experience, understanding, and training. To take this man or woman with all his limitations and lacks and build him into a teacher is a challenge to every whit of creative energy a leader has.

It is a good idea for the enlistee to spend some time in training before he ever takes a class, and many churches provide this opportunity through continuous training classes that meet at the time of the weekly workers' meeting. Whether such a class is available or not, the superintendent will use all the opportunities at hand to give the workers the special training they need. There are many such opportunities.

1. Printed Materials

There is no lack of helpful printed material available for training Junior workers. Free leaflets on every phase of work with Juniors may be secured for the asking from the Baptist Sunday School Board, Nashville 3, Tennessee and from the Sunday school secretaries in all the states. The two books in the Junior training course are required reading for every worker with Junior boys and girls. Our church library service recommends books for Sunday school workers, and in the periodicals published by the Sunday School Board instructive articles are constantly appearing.

2. Observing Experienced Teachers

In some Sunday schools a newly enlisted teacher is asked to observe for a few Sundays in a class taught by an experienced teacher. This might be a helpful practice if the teacher to be observed is carefully chosen, and if the teacher and observer have a chance to evaluate the lesson after it is taught.

3. Practice Teaching

This practice ties in with one of the soundest principles of education—we learn to do by doing. A teacher can read, he can observe—but he will not learn to teach until he teaches. It is a fine thing to allow the future teacher to serve as a substitute, to take his "internship" for a few Sundays. This gives him the feel of a class and helps to keep his feet on the ground.

4. Weekly Workers' Meeting

There is no finer training opportunity than the weekly workers' meeting. When teachers sit down together to plan a lesson, they think themselves into the Sunday morning situation. They discuss problems. They raise questions. A new teacher participating in this meeting gets a close-up of the practical aspects of his job not possible in any other situation. The experienced teachers are there to think through their problems with the new teachers and to do another thing, something that sometimes helps most of all—to share the fact that they too have problems not unlike those that beset the beginning teacher. (For a more detailed discussion of the weekly meeting, see chap. 8.)

5. Individual Guidance

Sometimes a superintendent finds it a time-saving, teacher-conserving practice to go over the lessons individually with the new teacher for a few Sundays. If a teacher is entirely inexperienced, he needs these private lessons to help him understand how to use his quarterly, how to make a lesson plan, how to use the Juniors themselves in the lesson procedure.

The superintendent can help through another kind of guidance. New teachers get discouraged, feel they are making no progress. The superintendent should be alert for signs that this is happening, and be ready to help a new teacher talk out his problems. Always it helps teachers, both experienced and inexperienced, when the superintendent notices and commends good work. A word of appreciation either written or spoken does much to revive a teacher's morale.

6. Meetings and Conferences

All Junior workers should attend their regular associational meetings and the Convention-wide and statewide clinics, training schools, conventions, and summer assemblies. Through these opportunities the worker gets not only practical help, but a vision of the broad sweep of his denomination's work, and renewed enthusiasm for his own part in this effort.

V. Who Should Enlist the Workers?

We have considered finding, enlisting, and training the workers. Now we come to a practical question, "Who enlists the workers?"

1. Enlisted Personally

Any one of the committee may enlist the workers. Since the Junior superintendent is the one who will work directly with the new workers, it is usually best for him to enlist the workers. He should certainly talk with them personally that they may know their responsibilities before agreeing to serve.

Sometimes the pastor, by a word of encouragement to the prospective worker, can help to swing his decision in favor of a yes.

2. Approved by Pastor and General Superintendent

In most churches the name of each new worker is referred to a committee for approval. This committee consists of pastor, general superintendent, and others. Whether there is a regularly-appointed committee or not, each prospective worker should be approved by the pastor and general superintendent. Having this reliable source of confirmation gives the superintendent security—and often may prevent an undesirable person getting into the Junior work.

3. Elected by the Church

All officers and teachers of the Sunday school should be elected by the church in its regular business meeting. This dignifies the office of Sunday school teacher and magnifies its importance. It gives the new teacher the feeling at the outset that his church is behind him.

VI. When Should the Workers Be Enlisted?

1. At Annual Election

It should be a policy understood by all that the Sunday school workers are elected annually to serve for the Sunday school year, although they may be re-elected and serve continuously for many years. Near the time for the election of the officers and teachers of the Sunday school, the organization should be studied, discussed, and necessary changes made. The organization then should be completed and everything put in readiness for the new Sunday school year.

2. Throughout the Year

When new classes and departments are added, or when officers and teachers must be replaced, workers should be enlisted. If a good worker is discovered and he is not needed at that time, he may be asked to serve as a substitute as he studies the work. Sometimes prospective teachers are asked to help with the Junior socials or to share in the parent meetings. The more these teachers observe and share in the work of the department, the more apt they are to line up with the department as workers.

Chapter 5

Men and Women at Work

Now WE ARE READY to meet the people who do the work of the Junior department, the men and women who teach and take records and visit and guide worship and do all the other jobs, big and little, that add up to a good ministry to boys and girls in the Sunday school.

How many men and women are needed? How should responsibility be distributed? What are the specific duties of each worker? In this chapter we will investigate these and many other questions related to the all-important subject of men and women *at work* for Juniors.

I. How Many Workers?

The number of workers required depends on the number of boys and girls—those already enrolled in Sunday school and the prospective members. There should be a teacher for at least every nine Junior possibilities or, even better, one for every six or seven Junior possibilities. (See chap. 3.) If there is just one Junior class in the Sunday school, the teacher must be more than teacher. He must be all things to the Juniors that a superintendent would be—the one person who represents their interests and welfare to the church.

But no Sunday school should be content with just one Junior class. If there are as many as five or six Junior possibilities, there should be two classes, one for girls and one for boys. When there are two classes, one of the teachers may serve as superintendent, and the other as secretary.

II. The Officers We Need

If there are three classes or four classes, there should be a fully organized department with superintendent, associate superintendent, secretary, musician, a teacher for every class, and two substitute teachers—a man and a woman. Some schools with only three classes have a fully organized department, and that is good provision for Juniors.

As a department grows, the organization should expand. Some schools have two and three associate superintendents, and one or more assistant secretaries. If a very large staff is needed, there are probably too many Juniors for one department, and the interests of that department can best be served by dividing into two or, if necessary, four departments. (See chap. 3.)

1. *The Superintendent*

An organization rarely advances far beyond the vision and ideals of its leader. The superintendent is the key to the effectiveness of the entire Junior organization.

(1) *Essential qualifications.*—Every one of the qualities suggested as desirable for Junior workers is doubly desirable for the department's leader. In addition, there are some special abilities, some over-and-above qualifications that a superintendent should possess for the simple reason that he *is* the leader.

Know the work.—In the business world there is a saying that the best executives are those who have "come up through the ranks." There is no substitute for the type of understanding a worker gains through first-hand experience. A superintendent is a better superintendent if he has learned the problems and procedures of Junior work "close up"—by actually working as a teacher in the ranks. But he should learn in other ways. He should read and read widely. All the denominational helps prepared on the subject of Junior work—leaflets, books, articles—should be studied and digested. A superintendent should keep abreast of constructive practices in secular education. He should observe, discuss, share the thinking of other leaders and teachers. Occasionally he may visit other Sunday schools. Of course he will try to attend the associational, statewide, and convention-wide meetings, where Sunday school methods are shared and discussed. The summer assemblies at Ridgecrest and Glorieta are two wonderful opportunities for the Junior superintendent to renew his vision and extend his horizons.

Like people and work well with them.—Since the superintendent works directly with so many different groups—teachers, parents, adults—it is essential that he be a mature, well-adjusted person who can work harmoniously with people—all people. Success in human relations is possible for anyone who honestly likes people, who is unselfishly interested in their welfare, who tries sincerely to put himself in another's place.

While being kind, sympathetic, and understanding, however, the superintendent must have—or cultivate—a balancing quality, the ability to stand firmly and resolutely for good work on the part of his teachers, to hold up high standards for everybody. Being kind does not mean being easygoing. It does not mean condoning poor work and overlooking failures. There is a term used to describe a quality teachers should maintain in dealing with Juniors, and it is a fine quality for a superintendent to maintain in his relations with the grownups he guides—"friendly firmness."

Delegate responsibility.—Getting others to share the work and enjoy the sharing is a mark of a leader. Some superintendents feel that they are proving their loyalty and their interest by taking upon themselves the full load of work and sparing the teachers all responsibilities possible. Instead of asking for help in such matters as preparing food for a picnic, planning a parent night, choosing colors for the walls, and so on, these "one-man" leaders try to do it all single-handed. Such leaders deprive everybody—themselves, the other workers, and the work itself. Two heads are better than one, and four heads are better than two. No single individual, no matter how gifted he is, can do a job as well as several individuals together can do it. There is another reason for encouraging the teachers' contributions to the work of the department. It is the best way in the world to get their interest, to tie them more closely to the work.

(2) *Responsibilities and duties.*—It is almost as hard to

enumerate a busy superintendent's duties as to enumerate a busy mother's duties—and for the same reason. Individual situations differ and the same situations differ from week to week. At one time or another, a superintendent finds himself performing every job in the department—and nearly every week he finds himself faced with some new and unexpected duty.

But there are certain fixed responsibilities that belong to *every* superintendent *every* week.

He is the leader of the department.—Whether the department goes forward, stands still, or goes backward, depends on the superintendent—his understanding and vision, his initiative and enterprise. A superintendent must know Junior work so well that he can continually appraise his own group's progress. Are the classes becoming so large that the individual pupils are not individuals to him and their teachers? Are the Juniors making decisions for Christ? Are the parents enlisted in the work of the department? Do the Juniors seem happy and interested—eager to participate? These are typical of the points which the superintendent will constantly check.

A real leader will, of course, be able to offer counsel and guidance to teachers when they have problems, when they need encouragement and practical help. By his own faith and optimism a superintendent will be able to inspire and encourage those who work with him.

Keeps a complete organization.—If, on Sunday morning, every class has a teacher, and if those teachers are the right teachers, the superintendent may well say to himself, "I have been true to my basic obligation." A good superintendent will not allow any class to remain teacherless. He will be prepared for unexpected resignations. This may mean having an associate teacher ready to take a full-time teaching place; it may mean having someone on the "future Junior teacher" list who can accept a class.

A vacancy anywhere in the organization should be of such concern to the superintendent that he literally cannot forget it until it is filled.

Supervises the training of workers.—Since Sunday school

work must be done by volunteer workers, the matter of training is a responsibility that the superintendent has with him always. He must not only develop the new workers, but must keep the veteran workers alert to their need for continual training. Guiding the teachers to printed sources of help—to leaflets, books, articles; maintaining a weekly meeting that is alive and vigorous; enlisting the attendance of teachers in the Sunday school meetings, those in the association, the state, and throughout the Convention territory—these are some of the opportunities for training that any superintendent has at his command.

Plans for the weekly workers' meeting.—It is the responsibility of the superintendent to see that the department has a meeting every week—but his responsibility does not stop there. He is responsible for this meeting being helpful, purposeful, and practical. The superintendent may enlist the help of other workers in many phases of the meeting, but the responsibility for maintaining this meeting and using it to give workers the help they need rests squarely upon the department leader. (For further discussion of the weekly meeting, see chap. 8.)

Plans for Sunday morning.—Sunday morning is the superintendent's own special time. He must guide the assembly program, but he must also oversee the many details of the organization. He must keep the session moving on schedule, and see that enough time is allotted to each part of the session. He must check and see that each worker is in his place and that the room by its orderliness, good arrangement, and choice of flowers and pictures at the front encourages the Juniors to worship the Lord in the beauty of holiness. Although the associate superintendent takes over many of the details of these matters, the final responsibility for a good Sunday morning is with the superintendent.

Commends good work.—Morale is an important factor in the quality of work that people turn out. A wise leader knows the power of an encouraging word to restore a teacher's spirit and enthusiasm and his will to keep trying. It means a great deal to a teacher, when he has made special effort, when he

has achieved something worth while, to have his superintendent say, either verbally or in writing, "I have noticed; I
am proud of you." Counseling the teachers, then, knowing
when to offer sincere praise, is an important part of teacher
training.

Provides needed equipment and materials.—As the leader,
the superintendent is in position to know what materials and
equipment are needed. He must see that the right lesson
courses are used in his department. Closely Graded Lessons
should be used if the Sunday school is graded, and Uniform
Lessons if the Sunday school is not graded. (See chap. 10.)

The superintendent must see that the space assigned to
the Juniors is the best the church can provide, and that the
assembly room and classes have the proper furnishings. (See
chap. 10.)

Extends Sunday school ministry into weekdays.—When
Junior workers have a right conception of their task, they
will see that Sunday school is not merely a *Sunday* school, but
that its values extend into all seven days. To see that the department has an adequate weekday program is the responsibility of the superintendent. If teachers visit and contact their
pupils regularly, if class meetings are held monthly, if the
department has social get-togethers for all the Juniors, if
frequent meetings of parents are held, if Juniors are encouraged to attend Vacation Bible school, then the superintendent
may feel that the department is doing a good work throughout
the week.

Makes evangelism a major goal.—Perhaps the superintendent's best opportunity in evangelism is to see that the teachers
understand their responsibility to win their pupils to Christ.
For it is the teacher, the *Junior* teacher, who is in the best
position of anyone in the church to win to Christ. In the
weekly meetings and elsewhere the superintendent may stress
this important goal of Junior work. He may lead his teachers
to study worth-while tracts on evangelism, and he may help
them through their study in the weekly meeting to find ways
to use the lessons to help Juniors become Christians, to point
out natural evangelistic opportunities in the lessons.

Supervises the program of home co-operation.—It is the superintendent's task to plan for parent meetings, and for observing Christian Home Week. He should enlist the help of the parents wherever it is needed—in providing transportation, in counseling regarding improvements, in contributing of their resources, in participating in programs and parties. By getting parents to use their talents, their skills, and their resources, the superintendent will insure their interest and enlist their co-operation.

Represents department in workers' council.—The superintendent meets with the pastor, general superintendent, and the other superintendents of the Sunday school in the regular meetings of the council. He should contribute his thinking to the total educational program of the church, at the same time, representing the interests of the Juniors and working to get for them all benefits possible.

Keeps department graded.—The experience of the years confirms the fact that Juniors are happiest and work best when they are in classes made up of their own age groups. It is the responsibility of the superintendent to see that each Junior is properly classified and placed in his own group, and that all Juniors are promoted every year.

Measures work by the Standard of Excellence.—The superintendent should see that every teacher measures his work by the class Standard of Excellence, and he himself should constantly apply the ten points of the department Standard of Excellence to the work of the department. In the weekly workers' meeting the superintendent has his best opportunity to use the Standard as a means to evaluate the work. The good superintendent will use the Standards in the right way—not seeking to attain the Standard just to be Standard, but perceiving in the various points a trustworthy measuring device for the quality of work that is being done in the classes and department.

Early in the year, when all the teachers have new pupils, the associate should take part of the weekly meeting time to talk visiting. Then he should check, week after week, until every pupil is visited. A very practical way the associate may help is by getting transportation for those teachers whose pupils live in a widely scattered territory.

2. The Associate Superintendent

This survey of the responsibilities carried by the superintendent will suggest that these are too many duties to be borne by any one officer.

(1) *Responsibilities.*—The superintendent needs a helper, an associate, someone who will share his leadership responsibilities, relieve him of some of his routine and detail work, and serve as superintendent in his absence.

In some departments there are two associates—in some cases, even three. In such situations the duties sketched below may be divided among these officers in any way acceptable to all.

Assists the superintendent.—A superintendent, like any leader, shows his leadership most truly in the quality of his creative planning, in his ability to look ahead, to dream dreams, to visualize improvements, and to find ways to realize those improvements. If a leader's time and energy are consumed in detail work, then he is wasting his higher talents, those gifts that originally qualified him for the position of leader.

The associate superintendent's first task, then, is to relieve the superintendent of as much routine responsibility as possible so that he may be free to plan creatively. His own eyes and imagination will show him what needs to be done. In addition to this basic task, the associate must assume responsibility in certain specific areas to guide the program of enlargement.

Looks for prospective Juniors.—This, of course, is everybody's business. Juniors, teachers, officers—all should bear on their hearts responsibility for the Juniors in the community who are not in Sunday school. But unless responsibility centers in some individual, the effort will not be purposeful, practical, or effective. In most departments this responsibility is carried by the associate.

His continual task is to keep the department conscious of

its enlargement-responsibility. When the name of a prospect comes to the department from any source—the census, or from some individual—the associate should get all the data necessary; then assign the name to the proper class. His task does not end there. He must check constantly to be sure that every effort possible has been made to enlist the prospect. This may take the visits of several different persons.

Encourages purposeful visiting.—How often does each teacher visit during the year? Has every teacher gone into the home of every pupil at least once? It is the duty of the associate to know; responsibility for the amount and kind of visiting done in the department belongs to him.

Serves as librarian.—If good work is going on in a Junior department—if Juniors are learning through creative activities, there will be materials and equipment of all kinds—maps, pictures, globes, chalkboards, books, story papers, posters, drawing paper, colored chalk, and so on. It is the duty of the associate to serve as custodian of these materials, to keep them stored and in good condition, and to issue them when needed.

The associate should see that quarterlies are on hand. He should make and keep an adequate file of pictures and encourage teachers to use the pictures.

Enlists attendance in workers' meeting.—Teachers should come regularly to the workers' meeting without reminders. But experience proves that whenever some individual assumes responsibility for publicizing the meeting, for sending reminders, making calls, and keeping the meeting before the teachers, attendance improves. The associate may do this work himself or get teachers to take turns sponsoring attendance at the meeting.

Sponsors training efforts.—A training school in the church or out in the association is the signal for the associate to go into action and give all publicity possible to that meeting. He may prepare attractive posters and mimeographed announcements. He may enlist the teachers personally.

The associate will create interest in state and Convention meetings and in summer assemblies.

Maintains an orderly attractive room.—The associate should assume responsibility for the appearance of the room on Sunday morning, for having flowers, for working with the superintendent to create an attractive center of interest (see chap. 6), for putting out songbooks, and for all the other details necessary to make the Junior rooms a pleasant place where it will be easy and natural to worship and study.

Plans birthday observances.—An important milestone—a Junior's birthday. It means a great deal to him and to his parents if his Sunday school recognizes the occasion. In addition to whatever the teacher does, it is well for the department to send birthday congratulations and to recognize the birthday in some way on Sunday morning in the department assembly. Most Junior workers feel that a once-a-month recognition of all birthday Juniors is sufficient, but others salute the birthday Juniors each week. Whatever form the recognition takes, the associate works to make this recognition interesting and worth while.

Greets and welcomes Juniors on Sunday.—There should be a host or hostess on hand on Sunday morning to offer friendly greetings, to welcome back absentees, to send visitors to their proper classes. This host not only creates an atmosphere of friendliness but can take care of emergencies caused by Juniors and late teachers.

Protects from interruptions.—During the assembly period the associate superintendent stands at the door to protect the department against interruptions or distractions. In this way he can take care of latecomers and visitors. He may also accept notices and announcements.

Enrols new pupils.—Responsibility for classifying and enrolling every member in the Junior department belongs to the associate superintendent. All questions pertaining to classification of the boys and girls should be referred to him.

Other duties.—Individual departments may add or subtract duties from this list. There may be a superintendent in charge of memory work, one who keeps the teachers reminded of their responsibility in this important area, who focuses on memory work in an occasional program.

In some departments an associate assumes charge of all home contacts—including visiting, parent meetings, enlisting the parents in special efforts.

Then again the associate may assume charge of contacting substitute teachers for Sunday morning. If teachers who must be absent contact the associate this relieves the superintendent of one of the most burdensome aspects of his work and frees him to give full attention to the assembly program.

3. *The Secretary*

Two qualities are desirable in a secretary, and they are qualities not always found wrapped up in a single individual. A secretary must be accurate, but he needs imagination too—imagination to see the human story the records tell, the faces behind the figures; imagination to share this record-story so graphically that the records come alive and challenge the boys and girls to achieve the purpose for which records are at work.

Two big responsibilities demand that the secretary be a confirmed clock-watcher on Sunday morning. He must be present early so that the classes may receive record materials and complete their records before Sunday school begins. He must work quickly to complete his work and share the record-story with the Juniors.

A good secretary will train himself to read the language the records speak; then translate that language into helpful counsel to teachers. At times records sound a warning: "Jerry has been absent three straight Sundays." At times they spotlight the good work of a teacher: "Mrs. Brown's girls study their lessons every week. She may be able to give us some good pointers." At times records are a searchlight illuminating weak, poorly developed areas: "Mr. Hall's boys rarely attend preaching."

The secretary's imagination and ingenuity are especially in evidence in record-sharing time on Sunday morning. When records are droned off in a dull, routine way, they have little meaning and serve no real purpose. But if the secretary plays up the human side of the records, if he sees and shares their human message, then they become constructive and helpful. The secretary may present the records visually—on chalkboard, chart, or some other device—or by playing up the "record high light for today," or by a guessing game.

The secretary will, of course, keep a complete, accurate, and up-to-date enrolment of the department. He will see that records are available at any time the workers need them. The best opportunity to analyze and share record information is in the weekly meetings and of course the secretary should attend regularly. Frequently part of the weekly meeting may be devoted to analysis of the records and to exchange of experiences and testimonies growing out of this study.

4. *The Pianist*

The pianist's work takes in so much more than accompanying the singing. His responsibilities include improving the quality of music in a department, guiding the Juniors to appreciate the highest and best in church music, increasing the range and variety of songs used on Sunday, discovering and helping to develop musical talent in individual Juniors.

The pianist must have some standards for music used in the Sunday school. He must be able to distinguish between worthy and unworthy songs—those that lift a Junior's thoughts toward God and those whose words are cheap or meaningless; between songs which convey thoughts a Junior might honestly express and those that are beyond a Junior's comprehension; between music that encourages quiet and reverence and music that invites shuffling, and stamping of feet and boisterous singing.

The pianist should, of course, be well trained musically. He should spend time learning to play for Juniors. This means knowing their voice range, playing the songs in the right tempo. The pianist should learn to play from memory the music most often used. This makes it possible for him to cooperate with the superintendent when some unexpected occasion demands a change in the plans for singing.

Above all, the pianist should be in his place for the entire session on Sunday. When the pianist carries another responsibility on Sunday morning, the superintendent is handicapped, the Juniors are deprived of one of their richest aids to worship, and the whole program suffers. For further discussion of music with Juniors, see chapter 10.

5. *The Substitute Teacher*

There should be a substitute teacher for every age group, preferably two for each age—a man and a woman. The use of substitute teachers is the only insurance a superintendent has against classes being taught by unprepared teachers.

Substitute teachers receive the lesson materials just as regular teachers do, and prepare the lesson every week whether they are called to teach or not.

A substitute teacher should visit the department frequently so that he may understand the purposes, get acquainted with procedures, and sense the feel of things.

Occasionally the substitute teacher should sit in a class when the regular teacher is present. In this way he gets acquainted with the Juniors, observes the regular teacher's procedures, and adjusts his own teaching accordingly.

Among the regular officers, the associate superintendent and the musician may serve as substitute teachers.

6. *The Teacher*

The very center of our Sunday school work, the vital core of its structure, is the teacher and his class. All the other work of the Sunday school exists for the purpose of helping the teacher help individuals. If the teachers are doing sound, vigorous, purposeful work, then the entire Sunday school will be in good health.

Because of the nature of his task, it is hard to set forth a specific list of a teacher's duties. The best teachers learn their duties not from textbooks, but from their own hearts. Love, understanding, and a high goal will show a teacher ways of helping he could never, never learn from a list of rules. The following list, therefore, will be only the barest outline, a framework on which the teacher will build as his experience expands and his wisdom matures.

(1) *Does an adequate job on Sunday morning.*—First, a teacher will be present unless unavoidably prevented. He will be at least as conscientious about his Sunday morning job as he is about his bread-and-butter job. No matter how fine the substitute may be, good classwork demands the presence of the same teacher from Sunday to Sunday.

The teacher will be in his place at least fifteen minutes early on Sunday, preferably before the first pupil arrives. He should have interesting and purposeful activities planned for these early Juniors.

The teacher will have an adequately prepared lesson. This means that he will have a purpose, one that seeks to bring about changes in what the Junior knows, feels, and does. It means that he will know the lesson content from study of quarterly and Bible. It means being physically fit and spiritually ready.

Remembering that pupils learn best by doing and that learning takes place best when the Juniors are interested, the teacher will teach his lesson through the use of interesting and purposeful activities, through getting Juniors to use their minds and eyes and hands and memory and imagination.

The teacher will know that he is responsible not only for the pupils attending Sunday school, but for their attendance in the preaching services. He will not be satisfied with attendance merely. He will work for attention during the services, for concentration, and for intelligent participation.

The teacher will plan his teaching period around the use of the Bible. He will help his pupils to know the divisions and books of the Bible as they come, to find its references, to memorize passages, to enjoy its study, and to use it—as a guidebook for everyday living.

(2) *Enlists new pupils.*—If a teacher believes in the purposes of the Sunday school—really believes—he will covet its values for all boys and girls, not for a favored few who come to his class. He will actively follow up all prospects, he will work to keep a missionary spirit alive in his Juniors so that they, too, may join in the search for out-of-Sunday school Juniors.

(3) *Visits the pupils.*—A good teacher will visit. He will visit to become friends with the Juniors and their families. He will visit to find life situations he may use in his teaching. He will visit to round out his picture of the Junior. He will visit to "talk Sunday school" with parents, to get their support and interest in the work of the class. He will visit for the reason every good friend visits—because he likes these people as friends and finds pleasure in contact with them.

And when will the teacher visit? When the pupil is new, when he has just joined the class. He will visit when there is sickness or trouble or sorrow in the family. He will visit the absentees. He will visit to share joy as well as sorrow.

(4) *Trains for the work.*—When he takes a class, the teacher should obligate himself to grow as a teacher. "We can never know enough to teach children a little." In any Baptist church a teacher has access to innumerable helps—free printed helps and others that cost a nominal sum. He has access to meetings that provide helps, meetings in his community and out beyond. He has access to discussion with other teachers in his own church.

(5) *Attends weekly meetings.*—The teacher should attend the weekly meeting not only for the help he receives in planning lessons, but for the help he may give. His thinking, his experience, his originality can be a vital source of help to other teachers. Attending the weekly meeting is one of the finest opportunities a teacher has to practice Christian stewardship.

(6) *Contacts absentees.*—The teacher must contact absentees each week—and contact them early. To wait until the end of the week to check up on an absentee is to show little concern for the cause of absence, and it may mean the loss of a precious opportunity to help in time of need. If the telephone checkup reveals some need, the teacher will visit immediately.

(7) *Organizes the Juniors for help in the work.*—Whether the class is organized formally or informally, the teacher is responsible for guiding the Juniors to contribute their abilities to maintaining a good class.

Chapter 6

A Good Sunday Morning for Juniors

It is Sunday morning and you, a Junior worker, are on the way to Sunday school. You hope it will be a good Sunday—that the Juniors will be responsive and interested; that the schedule will move smoothly; that the records will show improvement.

And yet you know that not one of these factors can be a complete measure of "a good Sunday morning." Juniors will be attentive if they are merely being entertained, and good records can be achieved for wrong motives. You must search more deeply for your standard, your measuring-rod. You must go back to basic purposes, those long-range goals we have set up for Juniors in Sunday school. Will the teaching of the morning, in class or assembly, help lift the Juniors' attitudes to a more Christian level? Will it lead some Junior who has not yet made a decision for Jesus to want to commit his life and heart to him? Will it deepen the Juniors' appreciation of God's Book so that he will be more willing to use it as a Guidebook for living? Will it lead some Junior to pray—really pray?

When you measure your work by ultimate purposes you will not always see immediately the result of your planning and effort; to know whether in the deepest sense your Sunday morning was "good." But you will have a trustworthy guide for planning, one that will help you move in the right direction.

As we explore Sunday morning, then, we will keep an eye on Juniors and our purposes for them. (See chap. 2.) We will look for ways to use each part of Sunday morning in such a way that workers may feel when the morning is over, "We really are a little nearer to what we want to do for Juniors than we were before."

I. Be Ready for the Juniors When They Arrive

Have you ever visited a home where you thought you were expected, only to find the doors shut, the shades drawn, the hostess absent? A spirit-dampening experience! When Juniors step across the threshold of their rooms on Sunday morning, they should read in the room and in the faces of the workers, workers already in their places: "You are expected; you are welcome; you are wanted." If the Juniors find a greeting like that, Sunday morning is really off to a good start.

1. *Let the Rooms Say, "Welcome"*

Is the appearance of the room an important factor? Sometimes we wonder. We work so hard to create a place of order and light and beauty for our Juniors—and they take it all for granted. Never do they compliment or even comment.

Yet the Juniors *are* responding—consciously sometimes, unconsciously all the time—to the atmosphere we have created. Juniors are concrete-minded. They have to learn of invisible things through the visible. The place where a child does his Sunday school learning influences his feelings about those learnings. A dreary, ill-lighted, cluttered Sunday school room will hinder, not help, us to teach the truths we want to teach about God and his Book; about Jesus and his way of living.

(1) *Good lighting.*—Good lighting is one of the elements in an inviting atmosphere. A child who said he did not like Sunday school explained: "It's because it always looks like it is going to rain in there." Dark rooms do something to the spirits. Outside light is best, and good provision for Juniors requires outside light for classrooms. Where outside light is insufficient, however, it should be supplemented by good artificial light—the kind that most nearly simulates natural light. A pin-up lamp may provide extra light needed if Juniors meet in a corner of the general auditorium where light is insufficient.

(2) *"Decently and in order."*—This phrase would apply to the arranging of rooms as well as to the guiding of new churches (1 Cor. 14:40). Piano, table, and cabinets should be free of clutter. Posters, charts, and signs that do not contribute to the purposes of Sunday morning should be off the walls and out of sight.

Chairs in the assembly should be arranged in an orderly way. The best arrangement is the one that encourages informal discussion, a natural give-and-take between superintendent and Juniors. If the room is long and narrow, the chairs should be turned so that they face the long rather than the short wall; so that there are fewer and longer rows. This is the place to say, however, that new Junior rooms should never be long and narrow. (See chap. 10.)

(3) *Something beautiful to see.*—But an inviting atmosphere is not achieved just by the absence of unsightly things. There must be positive effort to bring some beauty into the room. Beauty is achieved by pleasing colors in the walls, by the choice of pictures, by an attractive arrangement of objects at the front of the room, the "center of interest" toward which the Juniors look as they sit in assembly.

Every room needs a focal point, one spot which draws the eye, sums up the spirit of the room, or accents the theme of study for the day. We find this spot at the front of the room in the grouping of objects such as Bible, picture, flowers. Sometimes this grouping is for the sole purpose of creating an effect of beauty. Sometimes it is planned to catch interest in the theme of the assembly program.

For the center there must be a background. This might be a screen or a hanging of dark red or blue velvet. A white table against this dark background is effective. In many departments, Christian and American flags on floor standards are used on either side of the table. An open Bible, flowers on the table, and an appropriate picture on an easel behind the table, tacked to the screen or on a table easel, provide a satisfying grouping. If the Juniors are studying missions, the center might display objects from other lands. In a study of the church, a small model church might be placed on the table.

It is always an aid to good teaching to use, in the center, materials the Juniors have brought or made as an outgrowth of their lessons. If a class has illustrated a memory psalm or hymn, that would make an effective background. Just before Easter one class made a beautiful "stained-glass window" of black cardboard and colored Cellophane and contributed it to the center. Juniors may bring nature materials for the center—shells, greens, rocks, pine cones, wild flowers. Often the Juniors may work with the superintendent to plan and create a center of interest that is beautiful and meaningful.

2. *Let the Workers Be on Hand—Early*

But the human welcome is the important thing. When a friendly associate superintendent stands at the door to say "good morning"; when the superintendent signals greetings to the Junior from across the room; when, through the open door of his classroom the Junior sees his own teacher *already there*—then that Sunday morning has more than an even chance of being a good one.

Having the workers on hand does more than give the Juniors a good feeling of being welcome. It is insurance against boredom, against inactivity, against boisterous behavior.

3. *Have Activities for Early Juniors*

There is another way workers may say to Juniors, "We are ready for you": by having something for them to do from the minute they enter their rooms. This gives the Juniors a dynamic—not a static—welcome. These activities will be more meaningful and more purposeful if they are carried on under the guidance of the teacher. (For suggestions regarding early time, see chap. 7.)

But if teachers are not on hand, some provision will have to be made for the early Juniors. One idea is to have an associate superintendent, the pianist, or a substitute teacher engage the early Juniors in Bible quizzes, in recall of memory verses, in singing, or in memory-work activities. A word of caution: This should not be set up as a department policy, but as an emergency measure—something to take care of a situation that unfortunately happened. A good superintendent will constantly keep his teachers reminded of their obligation to be at Sunday school early—with activities for early Juniors.

II. EXTEND THE SUNDAY MORNING TIME

We certainly cannot have a good Sunday morning if there is not enough time to finish the activities we begin; if the teacher feels so hurried that he cannot take care of the Juniors' questions; if there is not time to relate the Bible passage to the Juniors' everyday experiences. One of our most obvious responsibilities is to do something about our too-brief Sunday morning time.

1. *Provide at Least 75 Minutes for Sunday School*

Many Sunday schools have only one hour for the entire Sunday morning session. Others have an hour and a quarter. Those extra fifteen minutes mean so much to the Juniors in Sunday school, and so little in the way of extra time at home. The best service a worker can render in the interest of more time for Sunday school is to try to get the Sunday school leaders to increase their time from 60 minutes to 75 minutes.

Fifteen extra minutes may mean the difference between bringing some classroom activity to a satisfying conclusion— and leaving that activity dangling; the difference between teaching a "facts" lesson and getting that lesson into life; the difference between having a share-the-news time in assembly and just dismissing the Juniors without extending greetings, welcomes, and the news of the records for the morning.

2. *Use the Early Time for Teaching*

By "early time" we mean the time before any scheduled activity begins, the before-Sunday-school time. In most schools many Juniors arrive at Sunday school ten, twenty, sometimes thirty minutes before Sunday school begins. On arrival at Sunday school the Junior should go to his teacher, and the teacher should make it a point to be on hand by the time the first pupil arrives and to start in right then with some activity relating to memory work, the unit, the lesson. If a teacher meets the pupils fifteen minutes early each Sunday, he has added thirteen extra hours to his teaching time in a year. (See chap. 7 for detailed suggestions regarding early time.)

3. Organize the Schedule Wisely

Another way to acquire more Sunday morning time is to organize the schedule so that time will not be wasted; so routine details will be handled more efficiently. Nowhere is stewardship of time more important than in the way we control our Sunday morning time.

What is the best way to organize this time? We want to use it for Bible study, for worship and fellowship experiences, and we want the Juniors to have these experiences in class and assembly. How much of their time should Juniors spend in class and how much in assembly? Which of these periods should come first?

Most Junior workers who have tried several plans now agree that the most practical one is to have the Juniors go right to class on arriving at Sunday school and to stay there throughout the class period; then come out for one straight uninterrupted assembly period. This means one continuous class period and one continuous assembly period.

If Sunday school begins at 9:30, such a schedule will proceed as follows:

9:30–10:15   In class
                       (Add any extra minutes acquired from
                       use of early time.)

10:20–10:45 In assembly

Having just the two periods eliminates the loss of time resulting from moving from class to assembly and from assembly to class. It saves something else—Junior interest or readiness. We all know that Juniors learn best when their interest is aroused; when they are ready to learn. But when we allow Juniors such short periods for study, they must often leave an activity just at the moment when their interest is aroused, and go on to something else in which they have no interest as yet.

If Juniors are to learn—really learn—they need longer blocks of time. If the teacher has the pupils in class for forty-five minutes or longer, he can complete some of his activities, can help his pupils come to some satisfying conclusions in their discussions. The same principle, of course, applies to assembly programs.

(1) *A problem.*—The one continuous assembly period brings up a problem. When should we introduce the fellowship activities—the greeting of new members, visitors, and absentees; the presentation of records; and the sharing of class news? Should these activities come at the beginning or end of the assembly? There is no rigid policy. They can be introduced anywhere, but most workers feel that they fit more properly at the close of the program.

(2) *Alternate schedules for Sunday morning.*—There is another possible plan for Sunday morning, one still followed by many schools. That is to have the Juniors go to class on arrival and to stay there for a ten-minute first-class period, to come out next for a first assembly period, to go back to class for a second class period, then out again for a closing assembly. While this is not the most desirable plan, it does have one advantage. If space is very limited and Juniors have little opportunity to move about in their class period, the frequent breaks in the schedule provide relaxation. Under normal conditions this four-session plan is not the one that encourages the best work.

One plan still followed by many schools should be avoided. That is the plan of having the assembly first with no provision for early-time activities. This plan not only wastes precious time; not only deprives the Juniors of the values of early-time activities, but means that some of the too-few class-time minutes must be given over to the taking of records. Records should be cared for *before* the class begins, so that the entire class session can be given to Bible study.

Taking everything into consideration, the two-period plan outlined above—the plan that allows for one class period and one assembly period—seems best. Workers who have not tried that plan should study it, evaluate its possibilities, and give it a try. In almost every case where that has been done, workers decide it is the one that best encourages real learning.

4. *Integrate the Morning Session*

There is another way to get more time on Sunday morning —and that is to plan so that the Juniors will get more value from the time they *do* have. One way is to try to make the Sunday morning session a *unit*, to see that the things Juniors learn in assembly supplement the things they learn in class and vice versa. Obviously Juniors have a better chance to learn when there is some unity in their Sunday morning activities. To lead them in the study of one subject in class, then introduce them to another subject in assembly, something entirely foreign and unrelated, is to ignore the principles of sound teaching.

This does not mean that the assembly program must directly parallel the subject matter of the lessons, but that the learnings in the assembly and the learnings in the class shall enrich and reinforce each other.

The superintendent may do this by enlisting the help of teachers in planning assembly periods, by relating his assembly themes to the lessons Juniors are studying in class, by using the assembly period for reviewing what is learned in class. This subject is discussed in further detail in section III below.

5. *Motivate Preaching Attendance*

There is another way to extend the Juniors' opportunities for Bible study and worship on Sunday morning, and that is to lead them to attend—and to participate in—the church services every Sunday. When we work to make the preaching services truly meaningful to our Juniors; when we find ways in class and assembly to enrich these services; when we seek ways to relate the Juniors' church experiences to their Sunday school experiences, we are making it possible for boys and girls to have two and a quarter full hours of Bible study and worship on Sunday morning, not just 75 or 60 minutes.

Over and over we should emphasize that Sunday school is

not really over for a Junior until the preacher pronounces the benediction on Sunday morning. We are happily getting away from the term, "We come to Sunday school and stay to church." We come to church. Sunday school is a part of the Sunday morning church experience, and the preaching service is another part.

As implied above, if church and Sunday school experiences are to flow together into a meaningful whole, we must do more than get Juniors to attend preaching services. We must help them to find meaning for their lives in each part of the church service, to participate, to concentrate, to go into the church service for a purpose: to learn, to find out, to explore. How may a superintendent do that?

(1) *Enrich the order of service.*—One suggestion is to help the Juniors understand better the meaning and purpose of each part of the service. Sometimes the church bulletin can be studied in the assembly. Or the order of service can be listed on the board and unfamiliar terms interpreted for Juniors, terms such as benediction, invocation, invitation hymn, prelude, anthem, offertory, and so on.

(2) *Study the work of the church.*—Assembly programs can be planned around a study of the church, the work of its officers, the pastor, the beginnings of the church, and so on. A good idea is to let the various church officers visit the Junior department and answer questions about their work. For example, Juniors might interview their pastor, asking such questions as: "How old were you when you knew God wanted you to preach?" and, "How many years of study does it take to become a minister?" "How do preachers decide whom they will visit?"

(3) *Discuss church experiences in Sunday school.*—Another suggestion is to discuss in the Sunday school session the things Juniors do and hear in the church services. Frequently the preacher's sermon mentions something Juniors have discussed in the lesson period. Sometimes his text is a memory verse, and again the Scripture lesson is a memory passage. Sometimes the congregational hymn or the choir hymn is one the Juniors have memorized. It is always interesting to watch

for such incidents and to discuss them in Sunday school.

(4) *Motivate attention to the sermon.*—Workers may find out in advance something of the content of the sermon; then ask the Juniors to watch for mention of certain facts. When such assignments are made, they should always be called for the following Sunday. Often Juniors may be led to write sermon reports—brief notes of a helpful thought or an interesting story in the sermon. Occasionally this activity may continue for thirteen Sundays; then the sermon reports presented to the pastor as a gift.

(5) *Magnify special days in church.*—Special church days, such as every-member canvass day, loyalty day, the beginning of a revival, can be highlighted in the assembly programs. On days the ordinances are observed or when Juniors are to join the church, or when deacons are to be ordained, the assembly period may make use of these events.

(6) *Use Bibles in church.*—Guide Juniors to open their Bibles and follow the preacher as he reads the morning Scripture lesson.

III. PLAN PURPOSEFUL ASSEMBLY PROGRAMS

A good Sunday morning, as we are discovering, is made up of many elements, but we have not yet touched the most basic one, the quality of teaching done in class time and in assembly time. This is the heart of the Sunday morning work, and it is the subject we are now ready to discuss. Because of the scope and complexity of the teacher's task, it is necessary to devote an entire chapter to that subject. In this section we will consider the assembly period.

1. *The Superintendent's Responsibility*

Responsibility for planning and guiding the assembly program rests on the superintendent. He may invite others to share in these programs, he may enlist the help of Juniors and teachers in planning for them, he may call on classes to contribute to them; but if the programs are to have purpose, continuity and basic unity, responsibility must center in some one individual, and the superintendent is the logical person.

2. *Purposes of Assembly Programs*

Every superintendent needs to face the question "What am I trying to do through my assembly programs?" Unless he has come to some sort of understanding with himself about the possibilities and opportunities which this period provides, he is apt to waste his time, to use it for activities that just entertain or fill up time. What are the superintendent's special opportunities?

(1) *To guide learning.*—Too many Junior workers think of the Sunday morning session as composed of two separate and distinct parts, each having its own unique function: the class period, which is for teaching; the assembly, which is for "presenting the worship program." This thinking is wrong. The activities of both periods should flow together. There should be opportunities for worship in both class and assembly, and there should be opportunities for Bible study—for basic learning—in the assembly as well as in the class.

The superintendent is a teacher, and perhaps his first responsibility is to guide learning—to increase knowledge, change attitudes, influence conduct. He does not have to duplicate the teaching in the class period. There are so many things our Juniors need to learn, so many areas in which appreciation needs to be deepened that it takes all the teaching both superintendent and teacher can do *together* to begin to widen the Juniors' understanding in such areas as prayer, the life and teachings of Jesus, doctrines, ordinances, how to use the Bible, how we got our Bible, what it means to become a Christian and live as a Christian—and many, many others.

(2) *To provide worship opportunities.*—The assembly time is not the only part of the Sunday school time when it is possible for Juniors to have worship experiences, but it is the time when they are most likely to have them. That is because the activities of the larger group—the singing, the praying, the listening, the quiet times, the offering time—are activities that especially invite worship.

Worship is a feeling about God, a feeling of being close to him, knowing he is near, responding to that nearness with a positive act of the will—thanking him, asking his help, resolving to please him, sitting quiet, and thinking of him. Worship is a thing that happens to a person; something that happens to his feelings, his understanding, his insight. Since worship is an *experience* and not a *program,* a leader cannot produce worship; he can only create conditions that make worship possible, can only provide means for the feelings of worship to express themselves in singing or praying or listening or dedicating of self, life, and talents.

So a superintendent's responsibility to teach goes beyond that of the teacher; he must teach so that his Juniors now and then—maybe one or more in every program—may have a genuine worship experience.

(3) *To foster fellowship.*—In every assembly period there should be some activities that foster fellowship and group spirit. If there are two assemblies, these activities should come in the closing one. If there is one uninterrupted assembly period, they should come at the first of the period. We may think of these fellowship activities as opportunities to share good news.

Good news of the records.—The sharing of records can be a happy and helpful part of the Sunday morning time— or a meaningless ritual. Records should be shared in such a way as to interest Juniors and challenge them to improve. (See chap. 10.) For example, the secretary may engage Juniors in a guessing game: "One of these numbers tells the number of Juniors staying for preaching," the secretary may say, writing two numbers on board; "and the other tells how many are going home. Guess which is which." Or "guess which class has the best record in 'Bibles brought.' One boy in Mr. Jones' class failed to bring his Bible. Guess what he is going to do about that next Sunday."

Some secretaries play up a "record high light" for the day. The high light may be one class that is 100 per cent for the morning. It may be a big improvement in church attendance, or a 100 per cent in "lesson study" on the part of boys. It may be new members or visitors.

Imagination in record-sharing time pays off.

Good news of class activities.—Good news is constantly turning up in the classes. Have new officers been elected? Has the class had a meeting or a picnic? Has somebody made a good record at school? All these events should be shared with the large group.

Good news from homes.—The arrival of new babies in the home, the good news that a mother, father, or Junior has recovered from an illness—all such items should be shared.

Good news about visitors and absentees.—The greeting of absentees and welcoming of new members is a happy part of good news time. The introductions may be made by the class vice-presidents or by the class missionaries.

3. *Sources of Programs*

There is one question most superintendents are constantly asking: "Where will I find practical help in planning my assembly programs?" In this section we will investigate that problem.

(1) *Printed helps.*—The beginning superintendent may need to use "ready-made" programs, but with increasing experience he will find that he is able to find his own subject matter and develop it as the needs of his own group dictate. There are many good books containing prepared programs; the superintendent may find titles listed in the Junior section of the catalogue from the Baptist Book Store. *The Sunday School Builder* also carries each month a unit of programs worked out for the use of Junior workers.

In addition to program books, every superintendent—both the beginner and the veteran—will need certain resource materials for enriching his programs, a few books that will provide an adequate "superintendent's bookshelf." These may be missionary stories, hero stories, biographies, Junior devotional books, stories of great hymns and great religious paintings. Titles are carried in the Junior section of Baptist Book Store catalogue.

Good ideas for assembly programs come from the superintendent's day-to-day reading—from magazines, religious journals, Baptist periodicals, the daily newspaper. Sometimes a happening in the community or town will provide a starting point for a good program. A good superintendent will keep alert for program ideas in all his reading.

(2) *The lessons.*—What are the Juniors studying about in their lessons? A good superintendent will know. He will go to the Juniors' lessons to find ideas for planning programs.

If a class is studying the life of Jesus, the superintendent may use his programs during that study to help them acquire additional background information—facts not covered in the lessons. He may decide on a unit of programs centering around everyday life in Palestine when Jesus was a boy— home life in Nazareth, the synagogue school, the out-of-doors world that Jesus knew, feast days and holidays, and Bible passages that Jesus learned.

Or the superintendent noticing that a class is to study the missionary journeys of Paul might get an idea for a unit of programs centering around Baptist mission work today. A unit of lessons on "How We Got Our Bible" might suggest a program study on getting acquainted with our Bible, in which the Juniors would have opportunity to find out more about the Bible's makeup, to have experiences in using it, and opportunity to search for rare and unusual Bibles for a Bible exhibit.

While the superintendent of a one-grade department or the superintendent of a small department using Uniform Lessons has a better opportunity to bring his assembly programs in line with the lessons, it is possible for any superintendent to do that—even those guiding two-grade departments or even four-grade departments. The close unity underlying the lessons of all four Junior years makes it possible to have programs closely related to the lessons.

(3) *Happenings in the Junior group.*—Things going on within the Junior group, events in which Juniors are interested, provide the superintendent with opportunities for building meaningful programs. When several Juniors have joined the church, the superintendent might plan for a unit of programs on the meaning of church membership or on what it means to live as a Christian. Right after Promotion Day there may be a unit on getting acquainted—with the

Bible, with the workers, with the Junior department, and so on.

Sometimes a single circumstance will suggest a need that can be met through a program. The department may acquire a new picture, a department Bible, new hymnbooks, or the Juniors may have moved into a new building. Through the programs the Juniors may dedicate their acquisitions and pledge to respect and care for them.

(4) *Happenings in the denomination.*—The superintendent has a unique opportunity, through his assembly programs, to help the Juniors acquire more knowledge and appreciation of their denomination. Sometimes meetings of the denomination—a meeting of the Southern Baptist Convention or of the Baptist World Alliance—may spearhead a program. Sometimes special movements or crusades may be studied, discussed and become an opportunity to learn and to worship. Special seasons and days such as Christian Home Week or Home and Foreign Missions Day suggest ideas for programs.

(5) *Happenings in the church.*—So many interesting things are constantly going on in a Baptist church, things Juniors should know about, appreciate, and share in. An alert superintendent will see in such happenings as a revival meeting, the signing of church pledges, calling of a new pastor, the beginning of a building fund or the dedication of a new building, the ordaining of deacons, observance of an anniversary in the church's life, the substance of an assembly program—or two or three.

(6) *Happenings in the world.*—Events of national and worldwide significance are often the starting point of an assembly study—such things as advances in the world of science and medicine, a national election, some new feat of exploration, and so on.

(7) *Seasonal interests.*—Of course seasons and special days—Christmas, Easter, Mother's Day, Father's Day, and others—suggest ideas for thoughtful and constructive programs.

(8) *Needs of Juniors.*—Sometimes problems that arise in the department suggest an idea for a group of programs—

problems such as irreverence or failure to attend church or absenteeism. Teachers and superintendent in their weekly meetings have an opportunity to face these problems, to think them through, and to decide together how they may use assembly and class time to work toward helpful solutions.

4. Principles of Assembly Planning

In planning and guiding assembly periods there are certain principles to keep in mind.

(1) *Begin with a purpose.*—We said above that a superintendent should have a clear-cut idea of his over-all purposes, a definite grasp of the function of the assembly programs. But he must also have a purpose for every unit of programs and for every program, a purpose much more definite and specific than the big general purposes. The superintendent should write out his purpose in terms of Junior experience, something he wants Juniors to know, to feel, to do.

(2) *Encourage Junior participation.*—In the assembly programs as in the lessons, Juniors learn by doing. The superintendent should give them opportunity to use their minds, to express opinions, to discuss ideas, to search their Bibles. A program that uses all the Juniors informally meets needs far better than one which uses a few Juniors in more formal ways—by the use of recitations, piano solos, and the rendering of memorized parts of a program.

A good assembly period, like a good lesson period, is marked by informality. The setting and arrangement of the room should be planned to encourage easy, natural exchange of ideas. The superintendent should be near the boys and girls; should stand on the same floor level, not on a raised platform.

(3) *Make wide use of Bibles.*—In the assembly periods the leader should give the Juniors many and varied opportunities to use their Bibles and to use them in meaningful and purposeful ways. Passive Bible reading, where the Juniors just read words, is not the most helpful way to study the Textbook of the Sunday school. Juniors should go to their Bibles to discover something, to find answers to problems, to square

their thinking with Jesus' teaching, to enjoy an interesting story, to compare their blessings with those of the psalmist, and so on.

(4) *Plan programs in units.*—Usually—not always—it is a good idea to plan assembly periods in units. When Juniors study a subject over a period of three or four Sundays, it is possible to realize bigger and more worthy purposes, to give Juniors opportunity to recall what they have learned, to carry out a project related to the unit, and so on.

(5) *Observe time limits.*—The superintendent should protect the teacher's time. Because of his smaller group, the teacher can meet individual needs more directly than can the superintendent with the larger group, and his time should be scrupulously respected. The matter of allocation of time should be worked out together by all workers in weekly workers meeting.

5. Deciding on Procedure

We will imagine that you, a superintendent, have decided what you want to do through your assembly programs; that you have now worked out your purposes. What next? The most interesting part of your work, planning your procedure, choosing the activities through which Juniors will be led to learn and to worship.

The list of helpful activities available for that purpose is almost endless. The assembly period is a fine time for the Juniors to discuss problems, search Bibles, sing, pray, listen to music, study pictures, think through problems, listen to stories, recall stories, help to tell a real-life story, share discoveries, find meaning in Bible verses, study maps, and to engage in many, many other activities. You will choose from the list those best suited to carry the ideas you want to convey.

You may be a superintendent who likes to begin always with a call to worship, and that is a good start for a program. Perhaps you will want a prayer next, or a song. Or you may decide to begin with conversation leading up to a prayer or a song. Sometimes an activity in the classes will start the program, or a problem arising from some interest of the class.

You will then plan the Bible-searching, the conversation, the story—whatever activities are to go in this program—in any order that seems best to you.

There is no set order in which the activities for a program should come. Often the superintendent departs from his planned procedure as he gets into his program. One thing he will seek to do always, and that is to provide natural opportunities for the Juniors to worship, through praying, singing, listening, and so on.

Programs vary, of course, but some activities are used in almost every program.

(1) *The call to worship.*—A call to worship helps the Juniors recognize their purpose in coming together, it reminds them that in a special sense, "The Lord is in his holy Temple." The call to worship might be a Bible verse or two (for example, Psalm 9:1-2; Psalm 100:1-2); it may be a song such as, "The Lord Is in His Holy Temple," or "I Was Glad When They Said unto Me," or a few lines from a familiar hymn, for example, the chorus of "Day Is Dying in the West." The call to worship serves a double purpose when it is a verse or two chosen from current Junior memory work. Psalm 67:3-4 and Psalm 96:8-9 are examples. The same call to worship might be used for three months or longer.

Prayers used with Juniors should be brief, voicing ideas that boys and girls might reasonably be expected to have, phrased in words intelligible to them. It is usually better for the superintendent to lead these prayers.

(2) *Prayer response.*—The prayer, even when led by another, becomes the Junior's own when he can share in it through a prayer response, either spoken or sung. The response may be the words of a Bible verse, for example, Psalm 19:14, a regular response from the hymnbook, like "Hear Our Prayer, O Lord," or a chorus such as "Into My Heart."

(3) *The offering.*—Whether the giving of his money is a routine act or an expression of worship depends upon the training the Junior has received in worshipful giving. For this reason an offering should be a regular part of Junior worship.

Through the use of offering verses, a dedicatory hymn, the enrichment of stewardship hymns like "Take My Life, and Let It Be," the Junior can be led to worship with his offering. Some appropriate offering verses are: Proverbs 3:9; Deuteronomy 16:17; Matthew 10:8b; 1 Corinthians 16:2; 2 Corinthians 9:7; Malachi 3:10; James 1:17; John 3:16. A suitable offering hymn is "We Give Thee but Thine Own."

Occasionally the leader might guide Juniors in saying a Bible verse silently just as he places his offering in the plate or in making a silent prayer.

(4) *The songs.*—Junior workers should hold high standards for the songs used with boys and girls. (See chap. 9 for full discussion.) They should remember that the hymns will be a medium of worship only as they guide Juniors' understanding of the words, motivate their appreciation of the music. "The chorus of this hymn is a prayer," the superintendent may say. "If you want to thank God for the blessings you just counted, will you sing it as a prayer?" Or, "See how many of the good gifts mentioned in this song God has given you, too." Or, "Our picture would make a good illustration for one of the hymns we are going to sing. See whether you can tell which hymn it is."

(5) *Worship opportunities.*—The high point of the assembly program comes when the Junior has experienced a desire to do something—to give his heart to Christ, to dedicate his talents, to study his Bible more diligently, to live more like Jesus, to share cheerfully with others. Opportunity should always be given Juniors to express these desires through some form of self-activity. If the program has centered on stewardship of time, the Junior may, through guided prayer or the singing of "Take My Life, and Let It Be," dedicate his talents to God; if the emphasis has been on evangelism, he should be given opportunity to think reverently of Jesus' love and sacrifice for him, then to make decision to accept him as Saviour; if the program's purpose has been to lead to a new appreciation of the Bible as God's inspired Word, Juniors might have opportunity to pledge allegiance to the Bible as an expression of desire to read it more regularly and to use it daily.

Chapter 7

What Is Good Teaching for Juniors?

It would take many chapters—actually, many books—to answer satisfactorily the question in the chapter title, and here we have *one* chapter in *one* book, too limited a space to get beyond the far outer boundaries of a subject so vast, so many-sided as guiding the learning of boys and girls.

There is in this series another book that does give teaching something of the space and detailed study it deserves. Readers are referred to *Better Bible Teaching for Juniors,* a companion book to this, for a more thoroughgoing treatment of teaching methods. All we can do here is to select certain broad principles of teaching and develop them in as detailed way as possible.

I. Preparing to Teach

When a teacher fails to do what he set out to do on Sunday morning, it is usually for one simple reason. He did not prepare. Some teachers will object to the diagnosis. "It was not my fault that things went wrong this morning, but Jimmy's," they will say. "I studied long and hard, but Jimmy acted up, kept trying to get attention—"

Wait. Isn't studying Jimmy, knowing something of why he has to have attention, planning activities that use up some of that surplus energy, a part of that teacher's lesson preparation? Studying the lesson does not mean studying the printed lesson only. Studying the Juniors, knowing the needs and problems of each individual is an indispensable part of lesson preparation.

Or a teacher may say: "I prepared a good lesson, but my Juniors got on my nerves today. I was jumpy and irritable."

Had she really prepared? Preparation of self—the physical as well as the mental self—is one part of lesson preparation. When a teacher fails to get the rest and sleep necessary for a relaxed and friendly relationship with his pupils on Sunday, he has failed in one basic phase of preparation.

Good lesson preparation means preparation in every area—preparation of self, preparation through pupil study, preparation through Bible study. In this chapter we will have space only for the last named phase—study of the Sunday school's textbook, the Bible.

1. Study the Unit

We teach Sunday school lessons in units. A unit is a group of lessons with a common purpose. A unit may have four or five or six—or even more lessons.

The advantages in teaching by units are obvious. A teacher can work toward bigger, more worth-while purposes when he has several lessons to help him than when he has one. In the course of a unit of several lessons a teacher has time to guide the Juniors in a piece of creative work—making a phylactery or a mezuzah, for example a scroll, or illustrating the events in a wall picture. When he teaches a unit, a teacher has a natural motive for helping the Juniors perform some meaningful service project, or to memorize a memory passage.

(1) *Survey the Unit.*—Since each lesson belongs to a unit, the teacher begins studying the lesson when he begins studying the unit.

What does it mean to study the unit? To look over all the lessons in that particular unit until the teacher has the subject matter in mind, to note how the lessons fit into each other and into the subject matter of the unit, to read all the Bible passages in order to get an over-all picture of the total Bible background, to study carefully the discussion of the unit and unit purposes in the teacher's quarterly, to survey the new memory work and the memory verses.

(2) *Decide on a unit purpose.*—In all this the teacher is studying *printed* materials. He teaches people, though, live, human materials. It is necessary, as he surveys the unit in the

quarterly, to take a good long look at his Juniors to find points where their experiences and these Bible passages touch each other, and touch the purposes suggested in the quarterly. "What problems of my own Juniors are suggested by this Bible material and the lesson treatment? What changes do I want to see brought about in my Juniors—changes in their knowledge, their thinking, their conduct?"

When the teacher decides what he wants his pupils to know, to feel, and to do as a result of all the lessons in the unit, he will have his unit purposes. (Many times the unit purposes stated in the quarterly do fit; other times they do not.) These purposes should be written down, studied, digested, and referred to in preparation for the study of each lesson.

(3) *Plan unit activity.*—Now comes a stimulating and enjoyable part of the unit study—deciding on some activity (or perhaps activities) for the whole unit, something for the pupils to do, activities that will get interest but, more important, strengthen teaching.

Maybe the activity most appropriate to this unit will be the preparing of a missionary or a Bible exhibit, the making of a map or a newspaper or individual notebooks or scrapbooks. Maybe the unit will climax with the writing of letters to missionaries or packing a box for some needy group, or a dramatization. Maybe a trip will be a fitting climax, a trip to a Good Will Center, a children's home, or to a synagogue to examine the articles of furniture Juniors studied about in the unit.

The big point is to clinch the learning in some active form of self-expression. It is an old maxim, but still true: There is no impression without expression.

Sometimes an activity will last for the entire unit, sometimes there will be several activities in the course of a unit. Teachers should remember that unit activities are chosen for their appropriateness to the unit, the possibility they have for deepening the learnings, and the appeal they hold for Juniors.

(4) *List the materials needed.*—Next, the teacher needs to list all the materials he will want to use in teaching the lessons.

He may need a map of Bible lands and a map of the world. There are pictures he will need, pictures in the lesson sets and pictures from other sources. He may need notebook materials, long sheets of brown paper for making maps, colored chalk, and many other items.

2. Explore the Bible Passage

One big advantage in teaching by units we have not mentioned; it is a time-saver, an interest-conserver. A teacher does not have to start out each Sunday morning on a cold trail to get his Juniors' interest. If he did a good job of introducing the unit, Juniors are already interested in some phase of that study—in discovering how we got our Bible, it might be, or finding out what it means to be a follower of Jesus, or learning what Baptists believe, or some other subject.

As he teaches each new lesson, the teacher's task is to build on interest created in previous lessons.

Does this mean that teaching by units releases the teacher from week-by-week study of each specific lesson? Not at all. The time saved is Sunday morning time, not weekday time. The teacher still must prepare a lesson every week, and preparing means studying the Bible passage carefully, prayerfully, studying the quarterly treatment, choosing a purpose for the lesson, and making a lesson plan.

Each lesson in the unit is based on a specific Bible passage, and studying this passage is the very heart of lesson preparation. The teacher needs to explore the passage to find God's message for him and for his Juniors. He needs more than understanding of the facts of the passage. He needs to have a feeling about the passage, to get it into his heart as well as into his head. The teacher gets the lesson, of course, but the lesson must also "get the teacher." Reading the Bible passage as his daily devotions for the week before he is to teach will help him share something deeply personal and truly meaningful with his pupils.

"Here is a little bit of God's truth which my pupils and I are going to explore together for five Sundays—a passage in which we will be sharing discoveries—" That is a good attitude with which to begin, an attitude better than: "Here is a passage that I am going to *present* to my pupils; here is something that I will *instil* into them."

We talk about the necessity for motivating our Juniors' Bible reading in order to insure purposeful study. Why not motivate our own reading—set up some questions that will guide us as teachers in getting all possible value from our reading? Before a teacher begins searching the Bible passage, he might ask himself four questions about the passage: Who? When? Where? What?

First, WHO are the people in the lesson? How many characters are mentioned in this study? We will try to identify each, recalling at least one thing we know about him. Who is the principal character in the lesson? What other facts does the Bible tell about him (or her)? How many things can we find out about this person from a Bible dictionary or a commentary? When we throw the searchlight of our study on *people*, they step out of the Bible and into our classroom on Sunday morning. They change from shadowy, long-ago figures to human beings, as real as next-door neighbors.

When we have the people of the lesson in mind, we might read this passage to see WHERE it took place. A story needs a setting, a background. We will find the location of the lesson on the map and mark it there. We will try to think of a good map activity for class time. We will consult a Bible atlas to find additional interesting facts about this place—facts about it today and in antiquity.

Then we will want to study the Bible passage to find WHEN the events took place. Was this a thing that happened at the beginning of Jesus' ministry or at the end? If it is an Old Testament story, we will want to know in what era of history it happened. Was it during the time of the Judges, the Kings, the Patriarchs? A commentary and a Bible dictionary will help us to place the events of the Bible in their proper sequence and a harmony of the Gospels will give the time of the events connected with the life of Jesus.

Then the teacher will read this passage to find WHAT happened, the events in the order they occurred. This means to get the feel of the story, so that the teacher could tell it vividly and interestingly if need be. Sometimes the teacher will tell the story while Juniors look on in Bibles, and at other times the lesson study will be Bible-searching and discussion. Whatever form the procedure takes, the lesson will have more reality and interest for the Juniors if the teacher himself has the story well in mind, its details and its climax. Reading the story in a good Bible storybook, will help the teacher.

3. Decide on a Lesson Purpose

Mauree Applegate, in her book *Everybody's Business, Our Children,*[1] tells of a twelve-year-old boy who had been so successful in teaching his dog clever tricks that someone asked for his secret. "First," he said, "I know exactly what I want my dog to do; then I figure out the way he'd like to learn it, and I teach him that way." He added as an afterthought, "My dog and I understand each other awful well, and that helps."

Almost every principle of good teaching is wrapped up in that twelve-year-old's formula. The boy succeeded, for one thing, because he had a *purpose.* "I know exactly what I want my dog to learn." A teacher needs to know where he is going in his work with Juniors. Everything he does in preparation for his lesson, the way he begins, the activities he chooses, depends on what he hopes to accomplish through his teaching. Too many teachers merely guide their Juniors in reading their "lesson" from Bible or quarterly, in discussing the facts of the lesson—and dismiss their class. They do not see the Bible lesson in terms of life purposes.

How does a teacher decide on a purpose for his lesson? He studies the Bible passage, he studies the printed purpose in his quarterly, he studies his pupils—and he studies something else, his *unit purpose.* That last-named factor is all-important. Every Bible passage chosen for Junior lessons is so rich in possibilities that a teacher is tempted to try to go in too many di-

---

[1] Mauree Applegate, *Everybody's Business—Our Children,* (Row, Peterson & Co., Illinois, 1952). Used by permission.

rections, to try to accomplish too many unrelated things in the space of a lesson. Referring to the unit purpose restrains a teacher from attempting too much in the space of a lesson, and it helps him remember the general direction in which he is headed; helps him choose from the many angles this lesson might take only those that steer his pupils toward the big unit purposes.

As suggested before, there are three kinds of purposes or goals that a teacher needs to keep in mind: What he wants his pupils to know—the factual information he wants his pupils to acquire; what he wants his pupils to feel, the attitudes he hopes they may be led to form; and the changes in conduct he hopes will come as a result of studying this lesson.

Someone has condensed this three-way statement of purpose into an easy-to-remember rule—Remember the three *H's*—something in the head (knowledge), something in the heart (attitude), and something for the hands to do (conduct).

One more thing needs to be said about purposes: The purpose a teacher chooses for one lesson will be more specific, more immediately attainable than the big, general purposes for the unit. If the unit is "Finding How We Got Our Bible," the unit purposes might be to help the Juniors know some of the processes God used to give us the Bible (knowledge); to help them grow in appreciation of the Bible so that they will study it more (attitude); to help them choose certain Bible rules to live by (conduct).

But for one lesson in that unit the purposes would be narrowed down. For example, the purpose for a lesson on "The Book God Gave" would be to help the Juniors learn from the Bible that it is indeed God's Book, to decide to read it daily this week, and to seek to live by one definite personally chosen Bible rule this week.

4. Make a Lesson Plan

A lesson plan is a picture in the teacher's mind of what he thinks might possibly take place on Sunday morning. Sunday morning does not always turn out according to the plan—in fact, it seldom does, for the teacher will adapt his plan many times to the needs of his pupils as they are revealed through discussion. But whether the teacher follows the plan or not is unimportant. What matters is making the plan.

We said a lesson plan is a picture, but it is not a still picture. It is a moving, living picture. It is a record of activities—things the pupils will do through which the purposes of the lesson may be realized.

A lesson plan does many good things. It saves ideas. As a teacher studies and meditates during the week on the Bible passage he is to teach, ideas come to him, good usable ideas with Junior appeal, and if the teacher is wise, he will put these ideas in a safe place, will insure that they do not get away. In other words, he will *write them down*.

Writing down a plan helps to clarify ideas. The very act of writing down our thoughts gives them shape and substance; makes it possible for vague wavering ideas to come through in sharper focus.

Writing down a plan helps the teacher to organize his thinking, to sort and arrange his ideas in an orderly way. This does not mean that he will, on Sunday morning, follow a set, rigid pattern, proceed in a one-two-three way. An activity jotted down at the end of the lesson plan might work its way to the beginning after the teacher gets into the swing of things on Sunday morning. And that good idea for a picture study may be discarded in the course of procedure. But having the ideas written down will enable the teacher to use the activities in the way that is right and natural.

A lesson plan is a written reminder—a little note *to* the teacher *from* the teacher—to include in this lesson the big important things—recalling memory work, making meaningful use of memory verse, searching the Bible passage, enriching its message with the use of pictures.

Having a lesson plan means that the teacher has thought through the procedure so carefully that he is better prepared to take advantage of the spontaneous opportunities for worship—praying, repeating a Bible verse meaningfully, having a quiet time or a listening time.

Most of all, a written lesson plan means that the teacher teaches what is his own; that the lesson bears the stamp of his own individuality. Maybe all the ideas come from the quarterly, but the very fact that the teacher has selected those activities, has arranged them in his own way, puts the stamp of his individuality on the "plan" which will bloom into a lesson on Sunday morning.

II. On Sunday Morning

Now we are ready to do some observing in the classroom, to go through Sunday morning with the teacher and his small group of six or seven Juniors. If it is right to make comparisons between one part of Sunday morning and another, we may say without apology that class time offers more opportunities for helping individuals than any other part of the Sunday morning time. The teacher with his small group can help individuals more specifically than can leaders of large groups; he can get closer to his pupils—to their inner life and their needs.

1. *Use the Early Time*

Some teachers do not know how to guide activities when the Juniors are coming in one by one. They have a set "lesson," which they are prepared to "present" at the appointed time, and so they waste the precious early minutes. Early time and lesson time should not be thought of as two separate sessions. Whatever is done in early time should further the learnings of the unit and lesson and the memory work.

Here are some suggestions from which the teachers may choose.

(1) *Activities relating to the lesson*

Making a chalkboard dictionary of unfamiliar words in today's lesson passage.

Studying the passage to decide how it might be dramatized. Some of the stories lend themselves very well to dramatization.

Working on assignments—finding from a clue written by teacher and given to pupils something in the Bible, in a picture, on a map, in the quarterly or source books on the class table.

Interviewing someone for information pertinent to unit—a church officer about his duties, the pastor, an elderly member of the church or a teacher.

Marking the location of lesson on map.

Marking references in Bible for today's lesson.

Looking up facts about characters we will "meet" in today's lesson. Finding date in a commentary, finding Bible verses from a concordance.

Answering thought questions in pupils' books.

(2) *Activities relating to memory work*

Matching pictures to verses in passage, then using pictures to enrich meaning and fix memorization.

Searching Bible passage to find ideas or word pictures as called for by teacher. For example, in studying Psalm 105 : 1-5, the teacher may call for the pupils to find the following: a verse that calls on us to be missionaries—verse 1; a verse that tells something we do in church each Sunday morning; a verse that tells something everybody should do every day; a verse that tells something we can do in our own neighborhoods and so be missionaries; a verse that tells who should have the most cause to rejoice.

Illustrating the memory passage or hymn.

Choosing from passage verses that will be appropriate for family table or hospital trays.

Studying passage to dramatize in assembly or to present as a choral-speech presentation.

(3) *Activities relating to the unit*

Making a map.

Working in groups on a wall picture that tells what the unit is about. Pictures may be drawn or assembled from magazines.

Making a model of the tabernacle.

Recording learnings in notebooks to be used as gifts.

Assembling articles for an exhibit—Bible, missionary, or out-of-doors.

Arranging lesson pictures in right order to show events that took place in unit.

Making a scroll, mezuzah or phylactery.

Early time is a good time to test the Juniors' understanding of what they have learned.

For testing knowledge of makeup of Bible, Juniors arrange books in Bible bookcase, use flash-card tests, or enjoy quizzes. For example, the teacher says: "I open my Bible and read the story of the Wise Men. What book am I reading?" Or he holds up a card bearing a Bible book and Juniors tell something about the book—if it is in the Old or the New Testament, the division it is in, the books on each side.

For testing recall of places, Juniors can mark on the map the answers to "Where did it happen?" Bright-colored tacks make good markers.

For testing knowledge of Bible characters, Juniors enjoy tests such as "Who said that?" and "Who am I?" "Who said, 'God is a spirit: and they that worship him must worship him in spirit and in truth'?" In the "Who am I?" tests, the teacher gives five clues as to a character's identity: (1) I was very rich; (2) People hated me because of the way I earned my living; (3) I had cheated many people in my town; (4) I was not as tall as other men; (5) I turned away from my bad ways after Jesus visited my home. (My name is Zaccheus.)

For testing understanding of memory verses, an "I see" picture game is good. "I see a picture that reminds me of the verse, 'Bow down thine ear, and hear the words of the wise.' What picture do I see?" To test pupils' understanding of the values of a verse, the teacher describes a life situation; then asks Juniors to recall a verse that would help the Junior faced with this problem.

(4) *Winning to Christ.*—Sometimes a teacher finds that the quiet of the early time period is an ideal time to talk to one or more pupils about accepting Christ.

In the early time the teacher can talk more personally to an individual than when the whole class is present. Sometimes a question in the quarterly can pave the way, or a verse in the memory passage. The teacher needs hearing ears for opportunities to guide the pupils' understanding of what it means to accept Jesus as Saviour and Lord and grow in ways pleasing to him.

2. *Get Interest in Unit and Lesson*

Ideally there should be no break between early time and lesson time. Activities begun in the early minutes, if they are relevant to lesson and unit, will lead easily and naturally into the lesson. For example, if the early Juniors worked on a scrapbook showing events in the life of Jesus, that activity has awakened interest in the life of Jesus, and now Juniors are ready to step right into study of the next "chapter" of this exciting story, and that chapter, of course, is today's lesson.

Since interest in the unit means interest sustained through the several lessons of the unit, the teacher needs to lay careful plans on the Sunday the unit is introduced. The main purpose of this opening lesson is to give Juniors an exciting taste of what is to come, to help them want to get into the study, to tackle it with zest and enthusiasm. Remember the twelve-year-old's second step in teaching: "Then I figure how he would like to learn it—and I teach him that way."

Figuring *how the pupils would like to learn it* is the most complex and difficult part of the teacher's complex task, but unless the teacher discovers this secret, there will be little learning.

One good way to arouse Junior interest in a new unit is to place around the room on Sunday morning interesting materials relating to the new study. If the Juniors are to begin a unit on "God's People Worshiping Through the Ages," the teacher might have on hand materials for making a model of the tabernacle. If the unit is to help the Juniors find how we got our Bible, the teacher might have on the table a collection of old or unusual Bibles, the starting point of a Bible exhibit which will climax the unit. Magazine pictures showing boys and girls of other lands might spark interest in a missionary unit, or a story map of Palestine might arouse interest in studying a unit on the life of Jesus.

Materials catch the eye, start questions, and provide something for the hands to start doing immediately. When eyes and hands and minds are busy, Juniors are well along the road to learning.

But on some mornings, interest in the unit does *not* carry over into the lesson. Often there are late pupils who did not participate in the early-time activities—or new pupils, visitors, returned absentees—Juniors who do not bring to the lesson study a good background of familiarity with the larger subject matter. So the teacher is usually faced with the necessity *every Sunday* of creating interest in the subject matter of today's lesson, of choosing a good interest-getter, an inviting opener for the lesson.

How can a teacher do this? A picture is nearly always a good springboard into a lesson, especially a picture of boys and girls in some believable life situation. Sometimes a life problem will wake up minds and whet appetites for the lesson. Sometimes a thought-provoking question or a true story or a little quiz or a personal testimony will pave the way to the lesson.

The thing to remember is that Juniors *want* to learn even more than teachers want to teach. If they seem allergic to Sunday school lessons, it is because the teacher has not found the key that will unlock the door of interest. But the key is somewhere, and it is so worth looking for.

3. *Guide the Study of the Bible*

The most outstanding difference between Sunday morning procedure for Juniors and for children younger than Juniors has to do with the Bible.

Juniors bring *their own Bibles* to Sunday school—and use them there. Primary children are not required to bring Bibles. The reason lies in the superior reading skills of Juniors.

When we say that Juniors use their own Bibles in Sunday school, we are not suggesting that Bible study for them is similar to Bible study in Adult classes. We must adapt our methods of guiding Bible study to Junior tastes, Junior abilities and interests. This means that we must observe certain principles in guiding Bible study with Juniors.

(1) *Motivate its reading.*—It is not enough just to guide the Juniors in reading their Bibles on Sunday morning. What they read must speak to their understanding, their experi-

ences. The teacher needs to build up interest in the Bible passage before it is read; then ask Juniors to open their Bibles for a purpose—to find, to count, to discover, to hunt, to compare, to match.

To say "Let's open our Bibles and read today's lesson" is not a good reason for opening the Bible. There is no challenge in that statement, no invitation to the thinking or the curiosity.

But let us imagine that the teacher has guided a discussion on great discoveries of the world; then suggests that the Juniors open their Bibles to Acts 10:28b to find a discovery as world-changing as any in history. (This would be Peter's discovery that every person—not just Jews—is worth while and important in the eyes of God.) Or perhaps the class discussion has been concerned with the right thing to do in danger, and the teacher suggests that the Juniors open their Bibles to Acts 21 to see which of their own ideas Paul followed.

Juniors may open Bibles to a passage to count their blessings or to compare their blessings with those mentioned in the Bible or to find in the Bible the same picture which the lesson picture tells or to follow someone on a journey to count the adventures.

Having a motive for opening the Bible sharpens the mind, insures concentrated searching, and gives point and direction to the study.

(2) *Interpret unfamiliar words and terms.*—A Junior teacher must be a Bible translator. The Bible was written for adults; many of its words and terms are beyond the understanding of Juniors. In addition, many of the terms in the King James Version have passed completely from our common speech. Yet the teacher must understand this book so well that he can adapt its language to nine-year-old level or twelve-year-old level.

This means the teacher must do what any translator must do—become proficient at two languages—that of the Bible and that of the Junior.

To aid him in understanding this Book, he needs some source books, a good Bible dictionary, a Bible commentary, a harmony of the Gospels, a Bible atlas. He needs, above all, to pray, to ask God to send him understanding, insight, and wisdom.

The other half of the translating job is important, too—understanding the Junior's capacity, his level of understanding, and the way he talks so that he may interpret Bible words in terms Juniors understand. How can a teacher do this? By living with Juniors, talking with them, listening to them, being friends with them—this will help the teacher to "think Junior" and to talk Junior.

(3) *Vary the way the Bible is read.*—In connection with guiding Juniors in Bible study, the teacher has a twofold responsibility—first, to help the boys and girls know the meaning of what they read; second, to help them feel that the Bible is an interesting, enjoyable book. To realize the second purpose, the teacher needs to use challenging and interesting activities in connection with Bible study, and to vary them so that Bible reading will never become routine or monotonous.

There are so many ways teachers can make the Bible come alive for Juniors. The group may read silently, watching for meanings suggested by the teacher. Or the different Juniors may read the words as dialogue. Or the teacher may divide the class into two teams and assign each team some things to look for in the passage. The teacher may list on a large pad or a chalkboard several questions relating to the passages; then read to find answers to questions. Or the teacher may give every Junior a Bible reference, ask him to read it, get it in mind. Then as he asks questions on the passage the Junior holding the verse that answers the question reads it.

Sometimes the Bible reading may be in the form of a cooperative Bible story. The teacher tells the lesson story as interestingly as possible, but pauses at certain points and lets the Juniors read the verse that tells what happened next. For example, the teacher asks Juniors to open their Bibles to Daniel 6 as she narrates:

> Far away from his own land, in Babylon where people worshiped idols, Daniel kept right on worshiping God. In a land where nobody prayed, Daniel prayed every day, reverently kneeling by his open window.

The king trusted Daniel and made him one of the three presidents who helped him rule Babylon.

This made the other two presidents jealous, and they plotted to have Daniel destroyed. Together they whispered and planned how they might find some fault with Daniel's work and get him into trouble. At last they thought of a scheme. (Teacher stops; Juniors read v. 7. Teacher continues story, stopping at certain points when Juniors will read Bible verses.)

Again the teacher may call for an impromptu dramatization. One worker, in teaching the parable of the talents, said: "Molly, you take the part of the first steward; Jean, you be the second; Helen, you be the third. Here are some pennies to represent talents. I will be the master who has just returned. Using the pennies, show me what you did with your talents."

Or the Juniors may make "living pictures" out of the Bible passages: "You be Philemon, you be his wife, you be the child. And, Joe, you be Onesimus the runaway slave standing in the door waiting for Philemon to read the letter. Then both of you say what you think the characters said."

Juniors enjoy *directed* Bible study. If the lesson happened to be Luke 15:3-7, the lost sheep, the teacher might suggest that the Juniors find words that tell how many sheep the shepherd left when he went looking for the lost one (v. 4); a word that tells how many were lost (v. 4); words that tell how long a good shepherd will search for a lost sheep (v. 4); one word that tells how a good shepherd feels when he finds his sheep (v. 5); words that tell what the shepherd asked his neighbors to do (v. 6); words that tell something that creates joy in heaven (v. 7).

(4) *Use visual helps.*—When Juniors have opportunity to use their eyes and hands as well as their ears in the lesson period, the learnings are strengthened. Teachers should have chalkboard and tackboard, pictures, maps, pencils, and paper—objects of all sorts.

These materials are well named "aids." They are not ends in themselves but aids to an end—helping the pupils understand and appreciate the Bible passage.

(5) *Use memory verse and memory work.*—The memory verse and memory work should be taught as part of the lesson. Since memory verses and passages are chosen for their close relation to the units of lessons, the teacher will find that any passage or hymn can be used one or more times in each lesson to reinforce or enrich the teaching of the lesson. For example, "Can you find in the memory verse a reason Dorcas was so willing to use her talents for Jesus?" Or, "Let's measure Joseph by the memory verse." Again the teacher may say, "Look at your memory work. How many reasons can you find for being missionaries?"

(6) *Relate the lesson to everyday living.*—We talk about the importance of committing Bible truth to memory. It is even more important to commit it to living. In fact, the Bible says that is the reason for having it in the heart—"That I might not sin against thee."

Over and over the Bible underscores the fact that having Bible truth in mind and heart is a means to an end—to changed hearts, changed living, changed viewpoints. We are to be *doers* of God's Word. Because Juniors in the First Baptist Church are accepting Jesus and learning his way of living, the sixth grade in our town and lunchroom and playground should be different places.

Juniors need to see this, need to know that there is a relation between their religion and such homely everyday things as washing the dishes cheerfully, doing their schoolwork conscientiously, finishing jobs they start.

Too often when the writer has guided Juniors in discussion on Sunday morning, she has found them able to give only two answers to what it means to follow Jesus—reading the Bible and attending church. *Those are two majors, two indispensables.* But religion is for everywhere, not just church. Religion is for all days, not just Sunday.

The most beautiful translation of the Bible is its translation into Christian thinking, Christian acting. (For further discussion of this point, see chap. 8, *Better Bible Teaching for Juniors,* the teaching book in this series.)

III. Testing the Teaching

After the lesson, the teacher should always go over his plan and appraise the results. Did the early-time activity really get interest? Was the Bible-reading idea helpful? Why, after this discussion, did the group get restless? Was the lesson too talk-y?

At the end of each unit it is a good idea to test the Juniors' understanding of what has been taught. A quiz or interesting test not only tests learning, but interests the Juniors. The teacher should test his teaching in another way. He should live closely to his pupils so that he may be able to determine whether or not the ideals and values of the lesson are changing their attitudes and conduct.

Chapter 8

More Than Sunday Work

WAS THERE GOOD ATTENDANCE in the Junior department last Sunday morning? Did the teaching catch interest, strike home? Had the Juniors studied their lessons? Did they attend the preaching service?

When the answers are yes, it is safe to say that work went on before Sunday—that telephones buzzed, doorbells rang, cards dropped into mailboxes—and that teachers prayed and planned and dreamed.

For it is a basic Sunday school law: If there is good work on Sunday, there has to be good work on Monday and Wednesday, on Thursday and Friday—all the weekdays.

I. STUDYING IN THE WEEKLY MEETING

The number-one opportunity to plan and pray and study toward Sunday morning is a weekly meeting of the teachers and officers. Because it involves time and an outlay of effort, many sincere teachers often ask, "Is it necessary? Why?

1. *Why Have a Weekly Meeting?*

There are so many reasons. Here are just a few.

(1) *To share problems, ideas, experiences.*—We talk about the importance of teachers knowing their pupils, but we rarely mention another related factor—the importance of workers knowing one another, enjoying a happy relationship with those bound together in a kindred task. When the Junior workers are welded into a friendly, sociable, co-operating unit—when they feel a strong group spirit—morale is higher, allegiance stronger, enthusiasm more alive.

This fellowship has practical value.

When workers exchange experiences, share ideas, "talk shop," they get a fresh perspective on their own work. When Mr. Brown learns that Mrs. Jones has discipline problems, too, he decides that maybe he is not a failure after all. When Mrs. Johnson shows the frieze her Juniors are illustrating as they study Psalm 8, somebody thinks, "Maybe such an activity will help my lessons." When Mr. Hunter shares his heart-warming experiences in winning an indifferent father to Christ, the workers thank God together and take courage.

(2) *To evaluate the work.*—If a Junior worker is to grow, he must be willing to stop frequently and take stock, to ask, "Honestly—how am I doing?" The weekly meeting offers a splendid opportunity to evaluate progress.

Through discussion.—The superintendent needs to evaluate his assembly programs. Teachers need to appraise their teaching. Everybody needs to look at the total program, face the problems, measure progress. Why is behavior in class-rooms sometimes rowdy? Could it be the fault of too-small classrooms? Or of late teachers? Why do all the Juniors not participate in assembly? Is it because the seating arrangement is wrong? What about the absentee problem? Is the program of the Sunday school ministering to the whole life of the Juniors? Are parents aware of the Sunday school's purposes—co-operating in those purposes?

And, above all, is the teaching of the department helping individuals to change and grow as Christians? Is Ellen a little more co-operative? Is Dick not quite so hungry for attention and limelight? Is Henry coming out of his shell, participating more happily?

The weekly meeting is the natural, logical opportunity for this sort of self-appraisal. The superintendent should ask for constructive criticism. Teachers should seek one another's opinions. Good evaluation means frank give-and-take and open-and-above board discussion among the workers.

Through record study.—The records provide a good starting point for evaluation. Once a month—or whenever there seems a need—the secretary should use the records to help the workers take a good long look at themselves. The records do what candid camera shots do—show up defects as well as good points. The true value of record study lies not in willingness to hear reports, but in willingness to face the weak places they show up and remedying them.

Through use of the Standard of Excellence.—The Standard of Excellence is another measuring rod. Constantly the superintendent should use it to gauge the status of the work, to let the workers decide whether they are providing a well-rounded program for the Juniors.

(3) *To pray for the work.*—If Junior workers did nothing else in the weekly meeting but pray together, it would be a profitable use of time. Jesus promised that group praying *changes things*. "If two of you shall agree on earth as touching any thing that they shall ask," he said, "it shall be done for them of my Father which is in heaven" (Matt. 18:19).

Vision, perseverance, dedication, patience—Junior workers need to pray for big, pressed-down, shaken-together, running-over portions of these. Our Juniors need so much praying for—and so do their parents and the work and the church and the whole program of the Sunday school.

To help her teachers recognize some of the areas in which group-praying might help, one superintendent prepared individual prayer lists for her teachers. Inside a "Praying Hands" folder she typed day-by-day suggestions as objects for their prayers—the parents, the Juniors, the lessons, the teachers themselves, the assembly programs, and others.

(4) *To plan for growth and improvement.*—When the Junior workers come together to "think Juniors," when their minds are tuned in to Junior channels—things are going to happen. Somebody sees a vision, somebody dreams a dream, "Couldn't we have more purposeful assembly programs if we divided into two departments?" "Wouldn't our teachers visit more often if they had small classes?" "Couldn't we have more activity if we put tables in the classrooms?" Questions like these wake up minds, sharpen insights, inspire suggestions that pave the way to improvement.

The weekly meeting is the time to chart a department visitation program, to lay the groundwork for stronger parent-teacher relations, to blueprint a better and more efficient pattern of organization. The weekly meeting is the time to call for reports on last Sunday's absentees and to follow up results of visits to prospects—and to do a dozen and one other things that add up to good work.

(5) *To improve the teaching.*—This is the basic function of the weekly meeting, and most of the time in most of the meetings should be spent in this all-important area.

What is the best way to help teachers improve their teaching? Usually (and notice the word "usually") by guiding them in planning their *own* lessons. This is a more practical and result-getting method than having somebody—even a highly skilled somebody—"teach next Sunday's lesson" every week. That is because teachers, like Juniors, learn to do by doing—not by watching somebody else doing.

But we said "usually." In some Sunday schools the teachers lack understanding of even the most basic principles of teaching, and if that is true, they are not ready to plan lessons. They need help in the ABC's of Junior work. If they have never studied the books in the Junior course, they should be guided in studying these. If the quarterlies are new and unfamiliar, teachers should get guidance in how to study and use the quarterlies. If terms like "memory work" and "early time" sound like foreign-language terms, then the weekly meeting is the time to interpret these basic phases of Junior work.

The principle to remember is this: Teachers ought to get in the weekly meeting the help they need at their particular level of development.

But when teachers do have a grasp of the fundamentals, they are ready to go on to higher levels of work. They are ready to plan their own lessons. But how?

A group in action.—Let's watch a group studying in their weekly meeting. This will be a two-grade department—one having nines and tens together. There are enough teachers in each age group to make a nice group for study.

On this night the Junior workers have met for supper with the other workers of the Sunday school, and now they have adjourned to their own rooms. Teachers of nines and tens have assembled for a brief time for a look at the work. A teacher led in prayer; then the secretary gave a brief report, comparing church attendance records for the last four Sundays and suggesting that superintendent and teachers do more to motivate church attendance in the assembly and in the class periods. Next the associate superintendent called out names of pupils who were absent Sunday and asked teachers to report on causes. Each teacher had checked on his absentees and was able to tell why they were absent.

Now workers have divided into two groups for study. Those who work with nines have gone to one table for study, and those with tens to another table. We notice that the setting encourages study. Lighting is good and on each table there are some reference helps—a commentary, a Bible dictionary, a harmony of the gospels, a Bible atlas, and a concordance. Each teacher has a Bible, a pencil, and a lesson plan sheet in hand. The lesson plan sheet, we learn later, was copied from one in the book *Better Bible Teaching for Juniors* and run off on the church mimeograph machine.

We decide to observe the workers with ten-year-olds. On the chalkboard the teacher guiding this study has listed the unit, the unit purpose, the lesson title, and the Scripture references for this lesson.

The leader starts by suggesting that the teachers put first things first: decide on a purpose for this lesson. They read the Scripture passage, consult the purposes listed in the quarterly, exchange ideas, and finally decide on a satisfactory statement of a purpose to write on their plan sheets. All the teachers, we notice, have gone over the lesson at home, some very briefly, others more thoroughly. Two have written out a plan.

Next teachers put their heads together to decide on early-time activities. One teacher says that her Juniors are illustrating the psalm they are memorizing and that she feels that this is the best use of her early time. Another says that since next Sunday is the last Sunday of the unit, he plans to use early time for a review. Another is readying a map game. As suggestions are made, teachers make notes on their sheets.

"How shall we begin?" This question brings forth vigorous discussion. Mr. Smith thinks that a picture will spark interest. Mrs. Owens decides that a question written on slips of paper and sealed will be a good "brain teaser." Mrs. Sims decides to write a thought-provoking question on the board.

The teachers, then, in turn, take up the various parts of the lesson as called for on the lesson plan sheet—how to guide the Bible reading, how to relate the lesson to life, how to make memory work and memory verse a part of the lesson. While there is not enough time to work out the lesson in complete detail, everybody has acquired several good ideas and the group-thinking has made the lesson come alive to the teachers and deepened everybody's interest in the Bible passage.

The workers have had about forty minutes for planning this lesson.

2. Facing the Problems of the Weekly Meeting

"A weekly meeting is not practicable in our situation." Many Junior workers believe that. The obstacles look so big and they feel so inadequate. How can they get teachers to attend? How can they guide them in planning lessons?

There *are* obstacles. But obstacles, you remember, are just "those frightening things we see when we take our eyes off the goal." With our eyes on the goal (and the goal is better Bible teaching for Juniors through group study), let us look at some of those problems and see whether we can think our way through them.

(1) *"Our situation is different."*—Not all groups can have a weekly meeting like the one we have just observed. There are very large churches and very small ones and churches in between. Some study Uniform Lessons and some study Graded Lessons. How can we adapt a plan to all these situations?

In small graded schools.—If the department we observed had been a department with four age groups and only two teachers for each age group, the matter of planning lessons would have been more complicated. Of course, if there are two teachers for each age group, and if there are *always two teachers* present, the thing to do is to break up into groups of twos. Two teachers make a fine study group.

But often there will be one teacher of nines present, and maybe two teachers of tens, one teacher of elevens, and two teachers of twelves. In this situation, the thing to do is to divide into groups, teachers of nines and tens studying together and teachers of elevens and twelves studying together.

While two complete lessons cannot be planned in the limited time available, a very adequate job can be done of surveying the lesson material in the two lessons and deciding on some good teaching activities. Both groups will find that this mutual study has widened their Bible background, given them good ideas, and provided a strong study-incentive.

Teachers will not be so concerned about "studying my own lesson" when they realize that the purpose of the weekly meeting is to help them increase their understanding of the Bible and improve their teaching skills.

There is another factor that makes it easier for two age groups using Graded Lessons to study together with profit. There is an underlying unity between some of the units studied by each age group each year.

In class Sunday schools.—In the class Sunday schools with only one Junior teacher, another problem arises. How can this one teacher participate in group study when he is the only one studying a Junior lesson?

This is a good place to say again: There should be two Junior classes, even in small schools, one for boys and one for girls. If there are two teachers, no problem exists; the two Junior teachers simply meet together to promote their plan and to plan.

But maybe the school does just have one teacher. Or maybe one of the teachers is absent. What then?

One possibility is for the Junior teacher to go into the larger group study. This study is usually led by the pastor, general superintendent, or an Adult teacher—and it is presented from an adult point of view.

However, the Junior teacher will benefit from participating in such a study. One complaint Junior teachers make is that they miss the stimulation of Bible study with other adults. This is their chance for that kind of study. There is another advantage: The lesson being studied is the Uniform lesson—most likely based on the same passage from which the Junior lesson is taken. The Junior teacher cannot share in the study of such a lesson without having his appreciation of the passage deepened.

Another idea, and perhaps a more helpful one, is for the Junior and Primary teachers to study together. At many points their work is similar. Both use music, pictures, memory work; both visit and both work with parents. By exploring the Bible passage with the needs of boys and girls in mind, each can contribute to the other's thinking.

(2) *"Who should attend the weekly meeting?"*—The answer is—everybody who works with Juniors on Sundays. The officers sometimes feel that the meeting is for those who teach, not for the one who guides the singing, not for the one who works with records, or the one who greets the Juniors.

That viewpoint is wrong. Every officer has a vital function in the weekly meeting.

The secretary needs to share the special knowledge he gleans from study of the records. The pianist needs to enlist interest in better music for the Juniors. Sometimes when a new song is to be introduced on Sunday, part of the meeting time should be spent in interpreting and teaching it to teachers.

The associate plays an important role in the meeting. He presents the names of absentees and checks with teachers on reasons for absentees. He checks up on the result of contacts with prospects. He arranges for teachers to visit. He directs the department program of visitation.

Then all the officers should participate in the study of the lessons. Since officers sometimes feel cheated out of the satisfactions of direct contact with Bible teaching on Sunday, this meeting fills that lack.

(3) *"How can we get the workers to attend?"*—See that they get help when they come—practical, usable help. Every teacher is hungry for good ideas. If word gets around that the

weekly group study is a place where they can get common-sense help, attendance will grow. The best advertisement in the world for any meeting is somebody's personal testimony that "the meeting is good. It helps me."

To get the workers started to coming, it is a good idea to send personal reminders, an attractive post card or a telephone call. Getting attendance is the associate's responsibility, but he may get others to help. One good idea is to ask different teachers to sponsor attendance on different nights. Teachers take pride in seeing how many workers they may get to attend.

Attendance is better if the workers have assignments, if the leader asks them to come prepared with good ideas for various parts of the lesson. One teacher might be asked to come with a good idea for early time; another, an especially good idea about how to begin; another, how to guide Bible study, and so on.

(4) *"My church does not provide a weekly meeting."*—In some churches there is no weekly meeting for workers; in others there is a monthly meeting only.

When the Sunday school does not provide a meeting, the Junior teachers should have their own. Some superintendents open their homes for the meeting, or suggest that teachers take turns having it in their homes. Where there is no meeting, Junior workers should try to arouse interest on the part of superintendent and general officers in providing one for the whole school.

(5) *"What schedule shall we follow?"*—What is the best time to have a weekly meeting? Usually the night the church has prayer meeting. This is a convenience to the workers.

As another convenience, many churches provide supper at nominal price, thus enabling many to attend.

Here is a possible schedule for the whole weekly meeting. It can be adapted to particular situations.

Supper	6:00
Promotion Period at Tables	6:30
Department Conferences	6:40
Prayer Meeting	7:30

The next question is, How can these approximately fifty minutes in the Junior group be best used? There is no arbitrary answer. The needs determine what subjects shall be discussed and the amount of time devoted to each. At times the entire meeting must be devoted to plans for some coming event, a parent meeting, a revival service, Promotion Day. But usually a schedule somewhat like the following is advisable. If, at times, the superintendent may feel that teachers need all the time for studying some special lesson, even the reports may be omitted.

Remember the principle: Need determines procedure.

Prayer
Record high lights, secretary in charge
   (four or five minutes)
Reports, associate superintendent in charge
   (about five minutes)
Planning the lesson (forty minutes)

II. WEEKDAY GET-TOGETHERS WITH PUPILS

It is important for many reasons that workers meet their pupils on weekdays, that they have fun together, play together.

Nothing a teacher can do demonstrates his interest in his class more vividly than his willingness to meet with them between Sundays. It is a powerful strengthener of the teacher-pupil relationship.

In addition, meeting pupils on weekdays is a way of saying that religion is for all days, not just one day.

But its great value is that a through-the-week meeting provides the best of all ways for a teacher to get to know his pupils—whole. It is not in home visits or in the Sunday morning class session alone that the pupil becomes a real person to the teacher. It is in natural situations—roasting wieners before a campfire, riding together, or playing ball.

1. *Class Meetings*

Teachers should meet with their classes at least once a month. (See section on class meetings in chap. 3.) Some teachers like to go beyond the rather formal "meeting," and make occasions to share their pupils' weekday interests in an informal way. They take them on tours and trips. They go fishing or sight-seeing. They play ball and have them in for spend-the-night parties, or for Saturday morning breakfasts.

It is surprising how many opportunities come up in these situations to discuss the work of the Sunday school class, to put feet under lessons, to discuss problems, to make plain what it means to be a Christian.

2. Department Socials

While the most important weekday meetings are teacher-class meetings, all the Junior classes should enjoy good times together occasionally.

Some schools try to have a social four times a year for the entire department, others feel that two a year meet the social needs of the pupils. Many workers find that a good plan is a party in the fall, another around the time of George Washington's birthday, an outdoor meeting in the summer, and a banquet for graduating Juniors in September.

If the department has parent meetings and plans good Junior socials in connection with these, this usually takes care of the matter of socials.

III. VACATION BIBLE SCHOOL

Vacation Bible school is a thirty-hour annual time bonus, and the Sunday school teachers and their pupils are the chief beneficiaries. The extra Bible study Juniors get in that school, the missions activities they engage in, the Bible passages they store away in their hearts, and the evangelistic teaching supplement and undergird the Sunday school teacher's work.

Junior workers should remember that Vacation Bible school is an extension of the Sunday school. Those who work with Juniors in Sunday school should work with Juniors in Vacation Bible school. If this is impossible, they should support the school with their interest and co-operation.

Chapter 9

Working with Parents of Juniors

IN THE PAST several years teachers have come to accept the fact that a closer relationship with parents of their pupils is a key factor in good work. Parent-teacher relations is no longer regarded as one of the "extras," something on the fringe of our program. It is an integral part of all good Junior Sunday school work, basic to its life and health.

I. THERE ARE REASONS

There are reasons why people who take their Sunday school work seriously have come to say, "We must work shoulder to shoulder with parents."

Teachers realize that children learn through experience, not just through listening, not just through memorizing. Listening and memorizing aid learning, but do not insure it. No matter how well a Junior has memorized Ephesians 4:32, he has not learned kindness, tenderheartedness, forgiveness until he has been kind, tenderhearted, forgiving.

Where does a Junior have the best opportunity to practice the values he learns at Sunday school? Not on Sunday morning, for Sunday school time is too short to permit wide and rich experiences in living. The home is the real laboratory for Christian living, for there Juniors have the time and the right situations and the two natural teachers, the two full-time teachers—father and mother.

When parents watch for ways to relate Sunday school lessons to everyday home living, then these lessons will be learned. But parents must know what their children are learning in Sunday school. And that is where home-church relations come in.

Teachers need to work with parents because what Juniors learn at home makes a deeper and more lasting impression on them than what they learn anywhere else. What parents believe and say and practice usually seems right to their children—more acceptable than what other adults say and practice.

Helping father and mother, then, with the spiritual guidance of their children is as much the work of the church as helping the boys and girls.

The fact that Juniors are still so subject to their parents is another reason for working with parents. If father and mother are just now-and-then attenders at church, it is hard for Junior to attend regularly. If the family car turns to the beach rather than to the church on Sunday, Junior is usually in the car. If mother and father read the Bible daily, if they use it as a standard by which to measure conduct, the Book grows in importance to the child.

We need to work with parents because our work at so many points depends on help at the parents' end of the line. If Juniors attend Sunday school regularly, if they are punctual, if they study lessons, somebody at home is usually working toward these same purposes, giving reminders, jogging memories.

II. There Are Ways

Many teachers who heartily endorse the idea of working with parents are baffled by the "how?" "We do not have space in our church," they say. Or, "We are a small church." Or, "We do not have funds."

A program of parent-teacher relations requires no space. It requires no money. It can be promoted in the smallest church. Working with parents does not mean doing something elaborate—putting on a function, having a banquet. Dozens of easy, simple opportunities for strengthening home-church relations are available to any Sunday school, no matter what its situation.

It is these opportunities we will investigate in this chapter.

1. Getting Parents to Help

This sounds roundabout. Do you not win people to your cause by giving rather than getting help? No, it works the other way. That to which people give their thinking, their toil, their energy, gets their hearts, too. When Mother hems curtains for the Junior windows or bakes cookies or fills her car with Juniors for the Junior picnic, she puts a little bit of herself into the Sunday school; she has an equity in its program.

There is no end to the types of jobs parents may be asked to perform in behalf of their Juniors.

Telephoning is one of them—telephoning parents and telephoning Juniors; telephoning to extend invitations or to give reminders.

Transportation is frequently a problem in carrying out Sunday school projects. Parents may be asked to use their cars to take Juniors to the picnic or the Christmas party or on a trip or to bring parents to parent meetings. Parents have even been asked to take teachers on their rounds of visiting. In one department a mother with a young baby, after taking a friendly teacher to call on her pupils one night, said: "It was such a relaxation for me. Tied down at home all day, it is a treat to take the car after supper and to see people."

Parents may be asked to use their skills—to decorate the rooms or letter posters or type invitations or take pictures or tell stories or lead a singing or bake cookies.

Parents have treasures which they will gladly lend for the enrichment of the teaching—a family Bible maybe for an exhibit, a piece of jade or a picture from the Orient for a missions exhibit.

Many parents have had rich experiences which they can profitably share with the Juniors. In one department a mother who had spent her childhood in Korea made a rich contribution to a Junior department by giving a vivid description of child life in that country.

Parents should serve their child's Sunday school in an

advisory capacity. If plans are under way for any changes affecting the Juniors—remodeling, redecorating, choosing new colors for walls—parents should be asked to serve on committees for making plans.

2. Reporting to Parents

Another home-church bridge is the report from teacher to parents. Regular printed cards are available at the Baptist Book Stores, and many teachers find them helpful. But some teachers feel that a personal note or word-of-mouth report has a warmer, more personal flavor.

Sometimes in telephone conversations or in accidental encounters with parents, teachers have a splendid opportunity to congratulate the parent on points in which the Junior has improved, and tactfully to ask for help in other areas.

A letter to parents, commending progress and pointing out areas to be improved is the best sort of communication.

DEAR MRS. MASON:

This note comes to tell you again that it is a pleasure to have Thelma in our class. Her attitude is friendly and co-operative. I am especially pleased by the improvement she has made in studying the lesson. For six Sundays now she has marked "lesson studied" on her record.

I believe that Thelma would get even more out of her Sunday school experience if she could attend church services regularly. Sunday-by-Sunday attendance at the church services is, I think, necessary to a child's Christian development.

If there is anything I can do to help you arrange this, please let me know.

Sincerely,

3. Using the Mails

Another way to build healthy relations with parents is through the use of the mails.

At the time Junior takes home a new quarterly, it is a good idea to drop the parents a note pointing out ways they may relate its teaching to home living:

DEAR MR. AND MRS. SMITH:

Yesterday Wanda brought home a new Sunday school quarterly. It would help so much if you would read this book through in order to understand something of what we are trying to do for her.

The purpose of the first five lessons in this book is to guide Juniors in understanding some ways they can make their homes happy. In each lesson you will find some suggestions for relating the truth of the lesson to home living. I hope you will watch for opportunities to help Wanda practice at home what she learns at Sunday school.

Often just reminding a child of something learned in a lesson can strengthen his decision to make a right choice.

Because our time on Sunday morning is so short, we need both of you as helping teachers through the week.

Sincerely,

The mails offer many other opportunities to talk to parents. When a new pupil joins a Sunday school class, the teacher should write a personal note, expressing pleasure at having him as a member. When a Junior joins the church, a letter should always go into the home. When a Junior goes away on his summer vacation, the teacher should keep in touch with him by mail.

Teachers should remember that every piece of mail going into the home, even if addressed to the Juniors, is also a parent contact.

4. Orientation Booklets

Some teachers take little booklets into the homes when they make their first visit there. The booklet, prepared by the teacher, extends greetings and explains some of the requirements of Junior work. It provides a way to conserve the values of the visit—to leave with parents the detailed information the teacher has given verbally.

One very attractive booklet prepared by a teacher of ten-year-olds was entitled "And Now You Are Ten." Bound with construction-paper covers, the book contained six pages. On the first there was a friendly greeting (handwritten) from the teacher, and on each of the following pages a few words of explanation under such headings as "Your Bible," "Your Memory Verse," "Your Memory Work," and "Going to Church."

A booklet prepared for nines was entitled "Now You Are a Junior." The words on the first page read:

DEAR DON:

My name is Mr. Cox, and I am your new teacher. I am glad you are to be my pupil this year.

On Promotion Day you will get a new name—Junior. You will like being a Junior, but you will find it is different from being a Primary.

On these pages you will find some ways Junior work is different. Please read all the pages.

The following pages explained the six points on the record, requirements about lesson study, church attendance, bringing Bible, and so on.

5. Class Meetings in Homes

When Mother straightens the living room in preparation for the meeting of the Busy Bees Class, when she gets out the punch cups and napkins and joins the group in its discussion and fun, she has become a participant in the work of this Junior class.

Class meetings anywhere are good, but when they are held in the homes of the pupils, they serve another value—one more link in good parent-teacher relations.

6. Newsletters

Many Junior groups prepare a monthly newspaper or newsletter. Activities of the classes, names of those achieving good records, reports of projects of all kinds are included. A newsletter serves to stimulate good group spirit. If mailed into the homes, it does something else—acquaints the parents with the work of the group and stimulates their desire to help their own children participate more fully.

7. *Printed Materials*

There are many fine leaflets prepared for parents. Some may be secured at no cost on request to the Baptist Sunday School Board at Nashville, Tennessee, and some are on sale at the Baptist Book Stores. These leaflets may be left in the home as calling cards when teachers visit. They may be given out to parents at parent meetings. The magazine *Home Life* may be given to parents who do not receive it through other channels.

8. *Class Mothers or Parent Sponsors*

Many teachers have found that the use of class mothers, or, better, parent sponsors (a father and a mother) is an excellent method for enlisting these appointed parents, and for getting them to enlist the aid and interest of other parents. These parent sponsors stand by to aid in problems, they help to get parent attendance at meetings, ask parents for the use of their cars when that is necessary, and enlist their help in securing needed equipment and supplies.

Parent sponsors may serve for three months or for six months. They may be chosen by the teachers or by the Juniors.

9. *Parent Meetings*

Any Junior group, no matter how small or limited its means, can have a good meeting of its parents and teachers. There is no need for elaborate plans and expensive entertainment.

(1) *Some long-range purposes.*—The important thing to remember is that parent meetings should serve some purpose. There is no value in holding a meeting to be holding a meeting.

Here are some valid reasons for teachers getting together with parents:

To give parents and teachers opportunity to get acquainted with each other and to talk together in a natural informal setting.

To help parents get a close-up of the Junior Sunday school program—to see the rooms, the equipment, the work the Juniors are doing, charts, and pictures—anything that interprets to the parents the purposes of the Sunday school.

To talk with parents about what the Sunday school is trying to do for their children and to invite their suggestions for ways the job might be done better.

To study the needs of boys and girls and seek ways parents and teachers working together can meet these needs.

To face the problems involved in Junior Sunday school work, and to invite the parents' help in working constructively at those problems.

(2) *Facing the problems.*—There are many problems involved in planning for meetings of parents.

How often?—There should be a parent meeting when there is need for one. In October when teachers have new pupils and new parents in their groups, a meeting is desirable. Parents and teachers need to get acquainted then, and parents need (and want) to know what the Sunday school is trying to do for their child and how they can help at their end.

A parent meeting in December or January is a good idea. By this time problems have come up, problems relating to the Sunday school program and to individuals, and it is a good idea to meet with parents for a frank evaluation of weak points.

In May when the emphasis in the churches and Sunday schools is on the Christian home, another meeting is in order, a meeting that will utilize the emphasis on family worship, Bible study, family church attendance featured so constantly during Christian Home Week.

By late summer, further problems have come to light and again a frank talking-through is helpful. Some schools have the summer meeting in the form of a picnic which teachers and parents prepare together.

But meeting-times are not necessarily confined to the occasions mentioned here. Good meetings can be held at any time. One group had a Christmas parent meeting in which parents and teachers (reinforced by a panel) shared with each other ways to make Christmas meaningful to children. Another group had a meeting with the workers of all the Junior organizations in the church—Training Union, Royal Ambassadors, Girl's Auxiliary, and Junior Choir—to discuss ways all could minister most helpfully to Junior life.

Who should come to the meeting?—Parents, Juniors and all the Junior workers should attend parent meetings. Juniors should be provided for in a place to themselves, and someone other than a teacher or a parent should be in charge of entertaining. The reason for this is that all the workers should be with the parents, and should participate in the group discussion.

Provision for Juniors.—One of the values of the parent meeting is that it brings Juniors to the church on a week night to enjoy a good time with parents and one another. Then, too, providing for Juniors makes it easier for parents to attend. Juniors may enjoy games, quizzes, a good film, a singsong. (The *Master Key Catalogue* lists titles of books giving suggestions for Junior parties and socials.)

The program for parents and teachers.—"What shall we do in the time when parents and teachers are together?" That is not the way to begin planning. The beginning point is the question, "What do we most need to talk with the parents about?" Sometimes there is need to share facts with parents; for example, at the beginning of the year, when the points on the record system are interpreted and the values underlying the records are highlighted.

If Juniors are not attending preaching services; if they are not studying lessons or learning memory passages—then workers should use parent meetings for a discussion of these problem areas.

One Junior group devoted one entire meeting to the subject of memorizing Bible passages, the necessity for it, the ways parents can enrich passages for the Juniors at home.

In another meeting the parents were given a list of values

that church attendance offers Juniors and asked to check those they thought valuable. The list included "opportunity to learn more about God"; "to learn how to be saved"; "association with people who honor God"; "a chance to be part of a big enterprise through the offering"; "training in worship"; "exposure to Christian atmosphere"; "understanding of the Christian way of life"; "helping solve everyday problems."

Next, parents and teachers discussed ways they might make church experiences more meaningful to Juniors. Suggestions included: Asking children to report at home on one helpful thought in the preacher's sermon; checking with other members of the family to see what they got from the sermon; deciding with the family how each could put into practice some idea from the sermon; sitting together as a family group in church.

Techniques for getting discussion.—Meetings with parents are valuable to the extent that they encourage the parents to participate, to think, to share creatively. A talk by some competent person now and then may be helpful, but it has one basic disadvantage: It puts the parents in a look-and-listen role. There are better techniques for getting parents to participate.

One idea is to break up into small groups, or buzz sessions, for consideration of some subject under discussion; for example, "How we can work together to get Juniors to attend church," or "Is regular church attendance necessary to a child's best development?" The leader raises the problem with the whole group; then suggests that the people sitting together turn chairs around so that they are in small groups. After "buzzing" for five or ten minutes, the groups pool their findings.

The advantage of the buzz session is that it breaks the ice, frees tongues, and permits more people to participate.

The panel is a good technique for discussion. The panel members do not make speeches but speak out informally as the discussion moves along. No law governs the number to be on a panel, but there are advantages in keeping the number to a minimum. Ten or twelve people are too many; whereas any number under six can be managed.

Sometimes the panel members are used as source people to be called on to clarify issues or to express opinions after opinions have come from the large group.

A film may serve as an excellent springboard into a discussion. Since the value of a film depends on the discussion it creates, it should be familiar to leaders before they show it. Pertinent questions based on the film, questions liable to arouse interest and cause discussion may be written out and handed to the group. Often the manuals accompanying the films contain discussion guides.

Sometimes a brief skit dramatized by the Juniors will pave the way to discussion. One superintendent wrote five or six short dramatizations, each highlighting some problem of interest to parents and teachers; then had the Juniors record them on tape recorders. Featuring such problems as regular Sunday school attendance, honesty, church attendance, living as Christians, and so on, these skits launched an interesting discussion on each topic.

10. *Visiting*

The oldest medium for getting parents and teachers together is still the best—the home visit.

(1) *Purposes of visits.*— Why should Junior workers visit? Because children are home-made. They are as they are because of whom they live with and the way these people live together. Until the teacher sees the child against the background of the home, that child never quite "comes through" in clear focus. In the home the teacher senses the climate in which the child grows—its spiritual, cultural, economic weather. In the home the teacher finds the factors that explain the child.

The primary purpose of a teacher's visit is to widen his understanding of the pupil. So he will go into the home to find out certain things. Are the parents Christians? Are they church members? Are there brothers and sisters? Does the mother work? What are Sally's interests and hobbies?

Does she like school? Does the home seem a friendly, livable place where children can be children?

Not all the information needed will come out in the course of one visit. Sometimes it takes several visits to get a well-rounded picture of the child. And not all the things teachers need to know come out from direct questions and answers. Sometimes the teacher needs to use his mental hearing aid to pick up incidental things, small but important things.

Teachers should visit to find situations they may use in their teaching. Peter has little sisters, twins; and Phil and his widowed mother live with his grandmother. These items will affect the lesson plans the teacher makes. Good teaching is always *personalized, keyed* to the individual.

Teachers should visit to share with parents the purposes and plans of Sunday school and to get their enthusiastic help. "Sunday school begins at 9:30. It is better if Sue gets there early. We start activities at nine." "We use our Bibles and a child is handicapped without one." "We believe that it is important for a ten-year-old to attend church regularly."

Teachers should visit to be friendly. The most effective visits are those motivated by simple friendship. Judy has had her tonsils out and her teacher takes her a bowl of custard. Stan was absent Sunday, and his teacher brings his quarterly over on Monday night. Sara has a passion for horses, and her teacher saves a beautiful picture clipped from a magazine.

(2) *"When should I visit?"*—A good visit is alive, productive, purposeful. It is sparked by the needs of human beings. It is different from the routine, perfunctory, "I've-got-to-go" visit as day from night. The routine visitor goes to discharge an obligation. The good teacher goes to explore, discover, build. The routine visitor counts times. "I've made two visits there and that is enough." But the good visitor counts needs. "Judy has been absent two Sundays. I had better investigate personally." Or, "Buddy's mother is coming home from the hospital today. I'll look in with some flowers." Or, "Instead of putting this new quarterly in the mail, I'll just drop by and deliver it in person. It

will give me a chance to talk to Phil's mother about memory work."

In our concern for the absentees, we should not forget the "presentees," those who are always on hand. Some teachers visit in the home of every pupil every quarter whether or not anything unusual has happened.

One question is always asked with regard to the visit: Should teachers drop in unannounced or should they telephone to say they are coming? Often consideration and courtesy demand that teachers call and ask whether a visit will be convenient at a certain time.

(3) *A program of visiting.*—In many schools a regular day each week is set aside as Sunday school-wide visitation day. Workers gather at the church (some in the morning, some in the afternoon, some at night) to receive names of prospects, absentees, and sick to be visited. The workers go out in groups to make the visits and later turn in reports.

The big value of having a stated time for visiting each week is that it keeps all the teachers reminded of their visitation-obligation, keeps the Sunday school visitation-conscious. Junior workers should welcome the benefits of such a program, share in and support it, remembering at the same time that it is always better for Junior workers themselves to visit the Juniors.

The most effective visit is—and always will be—that made by the individual teacher to the individual pupil, the visit that is motivated by love, concern, and genuine interest.

III. THERE ARE REWARDS

Maybe the best reason ever given for teachers and parents working together came, not from a teacher, not from a mother, but from a six-year-old boy. "Mother, he asked one day, "do you know my teacher?"

"No, Johnny," Mother had to admit, "I have never met your teacher."

"Then how," he wanted to know, "Can you both bring me up when you do not even know each other?"

Johnny had sensed a truth that two older and wiser people

had missed. Mother and teacher were both in the same business—helping Johnny grow—and that made them partners. Naturally, partners must work together, or their partnership will fail.

It is a little superfluous to urge teachers and parents to "get together" because they are together—together because of their common job, their common interest. What they should be urged to do is to share with each other— share their purposes, their hopes, their dreams, their thinking—and contribute to each other's efforts.

When parents and teachers do pool their hopes, co-ordinate their efforts, good things will happen for Juniors. Better Sunday schools will be one outcome, and better homes will be another. Juniors will have a better chance to grow strong in their beliefs and convictions, for the standards of home and of Sunday school will be more together. Juniors will have a chance to practice the learnings of Sunday school in the great school-of-life, the home.

Chapter 10

The Environment Teaches, Too

IT ISN'T JUST TEACHERS who teach on Sunday morning. Rooms and walls and space conditions and pictures and music—everything the Junior sees and hears and senses—is speaking to his mind and his feelings, speaking silently, but definitely, instructing, informing, teaching.

Because it is so important that these "silent teachers" say things that strengthen the work of the human teachers, Junior workers should study the factors that make up the environment, should see that they are helping, not hindering, them in realizing their purposes for boys and girls.

I. THE JUNIOR ROOMS

In every Sunday school there should be some space designated as the "Junior area." In size, shape, and location, this area will vary enormously from church to church. In some churches the Juniors will have a whole floor—four department rooms (one for each age) or even eight department rooms (two for each age), each with its own adjoining classrooms.

In other churches the Juniors have one department room for all four ages and in others, no separate room at all. They meet in a choir loft or in a church kitchen or in the pastor's study or in a corner of one room shared by other groups. No matter how inadequate the Junior area may be, it is important that it be the same place every Sunday, some fixed spot to which the Juniors always go, a place they call their very own.

A great deal can be done to change even an unpromising environment into one that encourages good teaching. A screen for pictures and maps can be provided even if the Junior space is only one corner of the room or one pew. In one small church the teacher of younger Juniors provided small boxes for seats so Juniors could use the pew as a table for their pencil and paper work. In another, where the Juniors met in a tiny vestibule, the teacher provided for each Junior a cardboard box tagged with his name. Inside the boxes, the Juniors kept activities materials and, when occasion demanded, also used them as lap desks.

1. *An Assembly and Classrooms*

The ideal arrangement for the Junior area is one assembly room (with sufficient classrooms) for about every fifty Juniors.

Good procedure for Juniors today calls for more and smaller departments than were once provided. The big assembly room surrounded with sixteen or twenty classrooms or a double-decker room with a main floor and a mezzanine is a thing of the past. Many churches have solved the problem of the oversized department room by partitioning this large room, thus making two rooms instead of one. In a double-decker room the mezzanine can sometimes be floored, thus providing an upstairs and a downstairs room.

2. *Arrangement of Junior Area*

Junior rooms should always be above ground and well lighted. Each classroom should have an outside window.

Entrance doors into the department should be at the rear or side of the assembly room. If doors are at front, they should be for exit purposes only.

Glass sidelights in walls between classroom and assembly room provide some natural light for the assembly room.

Rooms should be arranged so that Juniors face a solid wall rather than one broken into by windows and doors. This wall provides a background for a grouping of objects on a table, an open Bible, flowers, and pictures.

The number of classrooms for any one department should be in multiples of four, or an even number.

3. *The Size of Rooms*

Before we can answer the question, "How large should the Junior rooms be?" we must answer another, "What kind of activities go on in these rooms?" A Sunday school room takes its size and shape from the program carried on in that room.

If Juniors did nothing in their classrooms but sit still and listen, then very small rooms would care for them. Each child would require only enough space for the chair in which he "sat still while teacher instilled." Because Juniors learn by doing, however, the rooms in which they do their learning must encourage a wide range of activities—writing on the chalkboard for example, studying pictures on the tackboard, marking places on the map, completing unfinished sentences in their books, and so on. Sometimes in a twinkling, a Junior classroom changes into something that is a far cry from a classroom. It might be the throne-room where Paul testified before Agrippa, it might be Philemon's house, or the road going up to Jerusalem.

When teachers teach through activities, they need more space than when they teach through talking and telling.

It is well to plan for eighteen square feet of space per pupil in the Junior area. This includes assembly and classroom space. Since move-around activity is more important in classrooms than in assembly rooms, this space might be divided on the basis of ten square feet per pupil in the classroom and eight square feet in the assembly room. The large-sized classrooms, however, should not encourage large classes.

The absolute minimum that a church should provide for its Juniors is fourteen square feet per pupil, including classroom and assembly space.

4. *Shape of Assembly Room*

The assembly room should be large, well lighted, and rectangular in shape. A room that is too long for its width is not desirable, since the Juniors at the rear are so far away from the leader that participation in discussion and in other activities is impossible.

5. *Wall and Floors*

Walls should be of smooth finish plaster, painted in washable flat or semigloss oil paint with light reflecting value of not less than 50 per cent. Pastel colors are good in Junior rooms—green, rose, canary yellow, turquoise, peach (or a pleasing combination of any of these colors).

Floors and cove bases should be covered with linoleum, asphalt tile, or hardwood.

6. *Furnishings for the Assembly Room*

Furnishings for the Junior rooms should meet four tests: Are they comfortable? Are they durable? Are they functional? Are they pleasing to the eyes?

(1) *Chairs.*—Because they permit freedom of movement and encourage flexibility in arrangement of the room, chairs are better for the Junior assembly room than pews or benches.

Chairs for Juniors should be comfortable and should encourage good posture. A comfortable chair is high enough so that the Junior's feet rest flat on the floor and support some of his weight; there should be no pressure on the under side of the thigh at the front of the seat. The seat should slope slightly down toward the rear. Most nine- and ten-year Juniors will be comfortable in a chair that is fourteen or fifteen inches high. For eleven- and twelve-year-olds, chairs sixteen or seventeen inches high are recommended.

The legs of chairs for Juniors should be equipped with silencers.

(2) *Chalkboard.*—The assembly room should be equipped with a portable (not a built-in) chalkboard. A built-in board is a misuse of wall space. Not only does it mar the appearance of the front of the room, but it is not used enough to justify its constant appearance before the Juniors. A board that can be put away when not in use is much more desirable. Because they eliminate the old problem of dark areas and are more comfortable to the eyes, the new light-colored boards are more practical than blackboards.

(3) *Permanent picture.*—There should be at least one good

permanent picture at the front of the Junior assembly room. It should be large enough so that it can speak its message to all the Juniors, even those at the back of the room. It should be hung low enough so that Juniors may see it when seated.

Some pictures especially appropriate for Junior rooms are *Jesus and the Children* by Copping, *Christ in the Temple* by Hofmann, *Christ at Twelve* by Hofmann, *Hilltop at Nazareth* by Wood, and *The Smiling Christ* by Tom Curr.

(4) *Picture holder.*—The grouping of objects at the front of the Junior assembly room usually centers around a picture, one chosen from the lesson sets and changed from week to week. Some kind of holder for the picture is needed. This may be a small easel or screen at the back of the table. Many workers prefer a holder that rests on the table. A very nice one can be made from the heavy cardboard that reinforces the pictures in the lesson sets. When the corners are wrapped in leatherette paper, the pictures may be slipped in and out with ease. A cardboard leg is attached to the back so that it may stand alone.

(5) *Tables.*—The superintendent needs a small table for holding the materials he uses in teaching. For the secretary's use there should be a table large enough for convenient handling of his record materials. A table or shelf at the front of the assembly room is needed for holding the open Bible, the picture, flowers, and other objects which provide the interest spot toward which the Juniors look. (See chap. 6.)

(6) *Piano.*—Aside from its value as an aid to singing, a piano has many uses in a Junior department. It can help create the right atmosphere for worship; it can provide background music for early time; it can call the Juniors from classes; it can announce the beginning of Sunday school; and sometimes it can say, "Be silent, be silent," when discussion becomes boisterous.

The instrument for the Junior department should be a small one; this encourages ease of movement and allows the musician to see the leader and the Juniors as they sing.

(7) *Record player.*—A record player is a boon to any superintendent, but especially to one who does not sing well and

to one who has no piano. He can use recordings to teach a new song. He can use them to develop the Juniors' appreciation of truly good church music. He can use them to enrich programs at special times of the year—at Christmas and at Easter. And where a piano is not possible, a record player is a very good substitute.

(8) *Provision for displays.*—In the assembly room there should be some provision for displaying clippings, letters, articles, pictures, and other items of interest to Juniors. A tackboard may be built into the side wall of the assembly room for this purpose. For display of pictures, maps, or posters used in the assembly teaching, a portable screen or easel which can be moved to the front of the room is a good idea.

Tackboard and bulletin board should not be built into the wall at the front of the room.

(9) *Supply cabinets.*—Somewhere in the Junior area, in an entrance way preferably, there should be some place for storing of maps, posters, drawing paper, lesson books, and all the other supplies that vigorous teaching calls for. It is better if there can be two supply cabinets, one for Sunday school and one for Training Union.

(10) *Department Bible.*—A large Bible, open on the table at the front of the room, is a reminder that God's Book is the textbook of the Sunday school. In one department a large family-type Bible was used and in the blank center pages, the names of Juniors were inscribed when they became Christians—and the date when they were baptized.

7. *Furnishings for Classrooms*

Since Juniors spend more time in their classrooms than in assembly rooms, the furnishings for these rooms should be chosen with especial care.

(1) *Chairs.*—For the classroom, as for the assembly room, chairs are better for Juniors than fixed, immovable seats. Not only are chairs more comfortable, but they give the Juniors a feeling of being separate individuals rather than a class. In addition, chairs encourage freedom and informality in teaching.

(2) *Table.*—Good classroom work calls for a table large enough for the Juniors to work around comfortably. This table should be ten inches higher than the seats of the chairs and thirty inches wide. It should be long enough so that each pupil has about twenty-four inches of working room.

Where space is at a premium, some workers have solved the problem of the large classroom table by using folding tables, tables hinged to the walls and folded back when not in use, or lapboards. Some workers prefer two smaller tables which, when pushed together, make a table of the desired size.

(3) *Chalkboard and tackboard.*—For the Junior classroom built-in chalkboard and tackboard are desirable. Sometimes this may be a combination of the two. It should be about five feet by four feet in size, and two feet, ten inches from the floor.

(4) *Provision for wraps.*—A hook strip for wraps may be in the classroom within easy reach of the Juniors. In some departments the wrap space is recessed into the wall of the assembly room, and when this is possible, it is a convenience, since wall room is badly needed in the classrooms.

II. MUSIC IN THE JUNIOR DEPARTMENT

Whether music makes a worth-while contribution to the spiritual growth of Juniors or serves as a time-filler only depends on the Junior worker's understanding of its possibilities and the varied use he makes of it.

1. *Values of Good Music*

Music is an effective teaching aid. Listen some Sunday as the Juniors sing "Fairest Lord Jesus," "Holy, Holy, Holy," "Holy Bible, Book Divine," and "I Love Thy Kingdom, Lord," and notice the wealth of factual material these songs impart about Jesus, about God, about the Bible, and about the church.

Through singing, the Juniors have opportunity to thank God, to ask his special help, to pledge devotion to him, to resolve to live at their highest and best—to do all those things that add up to worship.

Singing is also a fine, relaxing activity. More important, it is an activity the Juniors can enjoy with others, with teachers, and with other Juniors. It fosters a sense of togetherness.

2. Some Tests

Since Junior workers have a definite responsibility to help the boys and girls appreciate the highest and best in church music, they need to be acquainted with some standards by which to measure the songs they use with Juniors.

(1) Do the words express thoughts that a Junior might honestly have? Of course there will be lines in some of the great church hymns Juniors use that will not be truly meaningful to them until they are older, but as a rule the songs Juniors sing should be expressed in clear, direct language with a minimum of symbolic thought. In such songs as "O Jesus, Once a Nazareth Boy," "Houses of Worship," "For the Beauty of the Earth," (all in *Songs for Juniors*), we find language that is right for Juniors.

(2) Does the music invite the Juniors to think reverently about God, about Jesus, about the Bible, and about the church? Or does it speak to the feet merely, inviting shuffling, hand-clapping, boisterous behavior?

(3) Do the words measure up to the highest level of Christian thought?

(4) Is there harmony of feeling and mood between words and melody? Does the music carry along the message of the words?

(5) Is the music within the range of Junior voices?

3. When We Teach a New Song

All the rules applying to guiding learning of Juniors in their study of Bible lessons applies to guiding their learning of new songs.

The adult who is teaching the song should, first, create a readiness for the learning; should build up interest in and appreciation for the words and music. Sometimes discussion of a Junior problem related to the song or the study of a picture will make a good approach to teaching the song.

Before they sing the song, Juniors should have opportunity to study its words, find meanings in them, discuss, suggest, question, comment.

The Juniors should hear the music two or three times before they sing it themselves. They may listen as an adult sings it or plays a recording.

It is almost as important that Juniors appreciate the music as the words. The leader should discuss the mood of the song, its arrangement; then let them listen to the music to find out if it "says" what the words say.

Next the Juniors should hum the melody with the accompaniment. Then—they are ready to sing.

Another thing to remember: Juniors' appreciation of a song will grow as they are led to sing it meaningfully. A prayer song should be sung as a prayer; a missionary song, to arouse appreciation of the church's work around the world; a praise song, to worship God. (For further suggestions, see chap. 5, "The Pianist.")

III. The Right Teaching Materials

Every conscientious Junior worker will want to know, "Are we using the right lesson materials for teachers and pupils? Do our workers and our Juniors have access to all the extra materials that are available for them?"

Of course it is essential that every teacher have a teacher's book and that every pupil have a pupil's book. To economize by giving the teacher a pupil's book only is shortsighted economy.

Not only do teachers and pupils need books; they need the right books. The Baptist Sunday School Board publishes two series of lessons for use with Primary, Junior, and Intermediate boys and girls: Graded Lessons, for closely graded Sunday schools; and Uniform Lessons, for schools that are not closely graded. In a school that has at least one class for each age in the Junior group, the Graded Lessons should be used; and in a school that has less classes than that, the Uniform Lessons should be used.

Beautiful pictures for enriching the teaching in class and

assembly are provided with both series. For teachers using Uniform Lessons, thirteen large pictures correlated with the lessons may be ordered each quarter with the lesson materials. Teachers using Graded Lessons find the lesson pictures in their own and in the pupils' books. In addition, large pictures (nine each quarter) are available for superintendents of departments using the Graded Lessons.

The weekly Junior storypaper *The Sentinel* contains a variety of material designed to enrich the Sunday school lessons—character-building fiction, quizzes, contests, puzzles, and many other interesting materials.

The monthly magazine *The Sunday School Builder* contains a section devoted to Junior work. It is important that every superintendent and associate superintendent receive his own copy. In addition, some Sunday schools provide the magazine for all their teachers.

IV. Using Records with Juniors

Taking records is of little value if Junior workers take them—and stop. Records are taken to be used—and they have many fine uses. Teachers should use them to show Juniors important areas in which they need to work for well-rounded Christian growth; to discover points at which these Juniors need help; to decide the direction some lessons will take. Superintendents should use them as a basis for finding out where teachers need help.

1. *Classifying and Enrolling Juniors*

On the Sunday he is enrolled, every Junior should be properly classified, then placed in the correct class.

To classify a pupil means to get his name, address, age, and birthday; then to record this information on the proper form (Form 10). The pupil should then be put in his correct class. Additional information on Juniors should be secured by the teacher as he visits the homes. (See chap. 3 regarding dividing line for enrolment.)

All new Juniors are enrolled the first Sunday they attend Sunday school. When the newly enrolled pupil is classified, he is taken to his class and introduced to the teacher. The teacher gives him the proper lesson helps and also explains the six requirements he should meet each Sunday. The pupil is not graded on the six points on the Sunday he is enrolled, but on the following Sunday.

The teacher should receive a copy of the classification slip on each pupil, and transfer its information to his own class-book. (*Junior Class Record Book No. 52* or *No. 53* is recommended.)

2. Securing Records on Sunday

Before time for Sunday school to begin, the department secretary should place in each Junior classroom the supplies needed for taking the records. This includes the class card (Form 30-Q) a sufficient supply of individual report envelopes (Form 15), and pencils for the number enrolled.

(1) *The department officers' report.*—Upon arrival each department officer fills out an individual report envelope and gives it to the department secretary, who compiles the information and makes the report of the department officers.

(2) *Report of pupils.*—Each Junior fills out his individual report under the supervision of the teacher. The teacher has an opportunity, as the pupil marks this record, to help him understand the meaning of each point and the reason for studying lessons, attending preaching services, and so on.

The teacher enters the record of each pupil (including his own) from the envelope to the class card (Form 30-Q); then to his own classbook. This classbook is the personal property of the teacher and should be taken home and used for reference in visiting and in lesson preparation.

A pupil who arrives after Sunday school has begun should mark his report at the desk of the department secretary and under his guidance. The secretary adds this report to the class card. He should see that the teacher has a record of this pupil's report for his classbook.

(3) *Class report and class grade.*—The class card with all the individual report envelopes (containing the offering), unopened, should be given to the department secretary.

(Many superintendents let the Juniors keep their envelopes and drop them into the offering plate during assembly.) The secretary should check the class card and total each column and compute the grade. To compute the weekly class grade, multiply the number for each of the six points by the amount given for each of these points, add these products, and divide the total by the number enrolled. The result is the class grade.

(4) *The report of the department.*—The results of the report of each class and that of the department officers should be totaled by the department secretary. The methods used in computing the class grade should be used in getting the department grade.

(5) *The report for the general secretary.*—The report of the department with the class cards, individual report envelopes unopened, and original copies of new pupils' classification slips should be sent to the general secretary's office.

A copy of the report should be filed in the department for permanent record, and a copy given to the department superintendent.

(6) *When pupils visit other schools.*—A visiting report card (Form 150) is offered for pupils to use in bringing back their record when visiting another Sunday school. Such record should be included in the pupil's individual monthly record.

3. *Interpreting the Six Point Record System*

ATTENDANCE—20 per cent. This point is self-explanatory; only those who are present shall qualify on this point.

ON TIME—10 per cent. Pupils shall be in the room in which they are to meet when Sunday school begins.

BIBLE BROUGHT—10 per cent. Bibles shall be brought from home. Since the New Testament is only a part of the Bible, it does not meet this requirement.

OFFERING—10 per cent. An offering shall be made at the Sunday school session.

PREPARED LESSON—30 per cent. The Junior will read the lesson material in the pupil's book and in the Bible; he will learn his memory verse, and make a reasonable attempt to do the written work in his book.

PREACHING ATTENDANCE—20 per cent. Pupils shall attend the regular preaching service of the church on the Sunday morning for which the report is made.

4. *Getting the Most Out of Records*

If records are to serve high purposes, certain specific things must be done.

(1) Records should be presented in an attractive, interesting way on Sunday morning so that they will come alive for Juniors, so that they will see faces behind the figures. (See chap. 5, "The Secretary.")

(2) Teachers should study the records of their pupils as recorded in their classbooks every week and seek to remedy the weak places they reveal.

(3) The department secretary should study the records, study with the eyes of his imagination to find the human story the records tell. Then he should share the results of his study in the weekly meetings.

(4) The records should be used as a basis for notes and cards written by teachers to pupils and to parents.

Yes, the environment teaches, too. Every factor that contributes to the climate of the department on Sunday should be studied by Junior workers, studied and weighed and improved so that even the inanimate objects will say: "Sunday school is a good place to be. Good things happen here."

QUESTIONS

Chapter 1

WELCOME, NEW JUNIOR!

1. What are some experiences that a nine-year-old undergoes for the first time when he becomes a Junior?

Chapter 2

WHAT ARE THEY LIKE—THE JUNIORS WE GUIDE?

1. Why is it important to begin a book on Junior Sunday school work with a close-up study of the Junior?
2. In what three basic relationships are Juniors changing?
3. What good purposes does the Junior "gang" serve?
4. In Junior years the need for activity is great. What does this suggest that Junior workers do?
5. Why is it so important to win Juniors to Christ while they are Juniors?
6. How can teachers learn about Juniors as an age group? As individuals?

Chapter 3

GROUPING JUNIORS FOR LEARNING, SHARING, WORSHIPING

1. In setting up a Junior organization, why is it so important to plan for the possibilities as well as the Juniors enrolled?
2. Why is it better to reach and win and develop boys and girls while they are Juniors than to wait until they are older?
3. What three factors should be considered in deciding how to group Juniors in Sunday school?
4. Why is it better to have small classes for Juniors?

Chapter 4

THE RIGHT WORKERS FOR JUNIORS

1. Look at the statement "The worker himself is the most important factor in the network of factors that make up Sun-

day school organization." Do you think that is true? Why?
2. What are some ways a Junior worker can cultivate his spiritual life?
3. Name four qualifications for a good worker with Juniors.
4. Name five good sources from which to recruit Junior workers.
5. What are some ways to train newly enlisted teachers?

Chapter 5

MEN AND WOMEN AT WORK

1. Name at least five responsibilities of the superintendent, the associate superintendent, and the teacher. Name at least two responsibilities of the secretary, the musician, and the substitute teachers.

Chapter 6

A GOOD SUNDAY MORNING FOR JUNIORS

1. Name two ways Junior workers may make the Juniors feel welcome, as they come in on Sunday morning.
2. Name five ways workers may extend the Sunday morning time and get more out of that time.
3. What are some good sources from which a superintendent may find ideas for his assembly programs?

Chapter 7

WHAT IS GOOD TEACHING FOR JUNIORS?

1. What four major things does lesson preparation involve?
2. Name three or four good uses of the "early time."
3. What responsibilities does the teacher have in guiding the study of the Bible in class?
4. Why is it even more important to commit the Bible to living than to memory?

Chapter 8

MORE THAN SUNDAY WORK

1. What are some values that come from a weekly workers' meeting?
2. What do you think is the most important thing to do in the weekly meeting?
3. Of all the ways teachers may find out about their pupils, which do you think is the best way?

Chapter 9

WORKING WITH PARENTS OF JUNIORS

1. Why is it so important to work with parents of the Juniors?
2. Name four or five ways teachers may work with parents.
3. List some methods for stimulating discussion in parent meetings.

Chapter 10

THE ENVIRONMENT TEACHES, TOO

1. Why is it so important to have roomy classrooms?
2. What are some desirable furnishings for a Junior assembly room? For a Junior classroom?
3. Name four ways to get the most out of records.

DIRECTIONS FOR THE TEACHING AND STUDY OF THIS BOOK FOR CREDIT

I. DIRECTIONS FOR THE TEACHER

1. Ten class periods of forty-five minutes each, or the equivalent, are required for the completion of a book for credit.

2. The teacher should request an award on the book taught.

3. The teacher shall give a written examination covering the subject matter in the textbook. The examination may take the form of assigned work to be done between the class sessions, in the class sessions, or as a final examination.

EXCEPTION: All who attend all of the class sessions; who read the book through by the close of the course; and who, in the judgment of the teacher, do the classwork satisfactorily may be exempted from taking the examination.

4. Application for Sunday school awards should be sent to the state Sunday school department on proper application forms. These forms should be made in triplicate. Keep the last copy for the church file, and send the other two copies.

II. DIRECTIONS FOR THE STUDENT *

1. *In Classwork*

(1) The student must attend at least six of the ten forty-five minute class periods to be entitled to take the class examination.

(2) The student must certify that the textbook has been read. (In rare cases where students may find it impracticable to read the book before the completion of the classwork, the teacher may accept a promise to read the book carefully

---

* The student must be fifteen years of age or older to receive Sunday school credit.

within the next two weeks. This applies only to students who do the written work.)

(3) The student must take a written examination, making a minimum grade of 70 per cent, or qualify according to *Exception* noted above.

2. *In Individual Study by Correspondence*

Those who for any reason wish to study the book without the guidance of a teacher will use one of the following methods:

(1) Write answers to the questions printed in the book, or

(2) Write a summary of each chapter or a development of the chapter outlines.

In either case the student must read the book through.

Students may find profit in studying the text together, but where awards are requested, individual papers are required. Carbon copies or duplicates in any form cannot be accepted.

All written work done by such students on books for Sunday school credit should be sent to the Sunday school secretary.

III. THIS BOOK GIVES CREDIT IN SECTION V OF THE SUNDAY SCHOOL TRAINING COURSE.